A PICTORIAL
HISTORY OF OUR
ENGLISH BIBLE

A PICTORIAL
HISTORY OF OUR
ENGLISH BIBLE

DAVID BEALE

BJU PRESS

GREENVILLE, SOUTH CAROLINA

The Library of Congress has cataloged the first printing of this title as follows:

Beale, David, 1944-
  A pictorial history of our English Bible / David Beale. —
Greenville, S.C.: Bob Jones University Press, c1982.

  73 p. : ill. ; 22 cm.
  Bibliography: p. 69-70.
  Includes index.
  ISBN 0-89084-149-7 (pbk.)

  1. Bible. English—Versions. I. Title.
BS455.B38 1982   220.5'2'009—dc19   83-198172
                                                    AACR 2 MARC

All Scripture is quoted from the Authorized King James Version unless otherwise noted.

A Pictorial History of Our English Bible
David Beale

Cover: Unusual Films
Cover design: Olaf Ebert

©1982 Bob Jones University Press
Greenville, South Carolina 29614

ISBN 0-89084-149-7

15 14 13 12 11 10 9 8 7

Contents

Table of Illustrations

Photographs by Dan Calnon/Unusual Films

Introduction

The Bible is the absolute, infallible and inerrant Word of God—the special revelation of God to man. Its message and contents move inerrantly through the framework of human history and speak of the most profound scientific facts in a casual manner: "He stretcheth out the north over the empty place, and hangeth the earth upon nothing," remarks Job (26:7). The humble fisherman, Peter, correctly speaks of the elements of the universe: "The heavens shall pass away with a great noise, and the elements shall melt with fervent heat" (II Peter 3:10).

In an inexplicable manner, the Holy Spirit inspired (outbreathed) the original autographs of the 66 Scripture books (II Timothy 3:16). He guided the Scripture writers in the selection of the materials which they used (Luke 1:1-4) and even in the choice of the words which they employed (II Peter 1:20-21). God used men to write a book which is essentially divine; He used the writers' individual vocabularies, styles, and experiences to express precisely what He wanted to reveal to man. God not only inspired all Scripture, but He inspired all Scripture equally; conservative theologians refer to this as *verbal plenary inspiration.* God kept the Scripture writers from all error and from all omission (Deuteronomy 4:2; John 10:35).

Although a 66-book "library," the Bible is essentially one book, forming one continuous story, bearing witness to one God, revealing one plan of redemption and

The Isaiah Scroll. One of the best-preserved of the nearly 600 manuscripts found in the Qumran caves, on the Israeli-occupied West Bank of the Dead Sea, in 1947. This is one of the oldest Hebrew manuscripts known to exist.

unfolding one grand central theme—the person and work of the Lord Jesus Christ (Luke 24:25-27; John 5:39, 46).

The 39 Old Testament Books

The word *testament* means "covenant" or "agreement," and the Scriptures use the term to designate the relationship which exists between God and His people. The Old Testament was written in Hebrew except for portions of Daniel and Ezra which were written in Aramaic. Most of the writers remained in Israel as they penned their works; the most notable exceptions were Daniel and Ezekiel who wrote from Babylon, and Jeremiah who wrote parts of his work from Egypt.

The Old Testament writers completed their 39 books over a period of about 1500 years. By Ezra's day (fifth century B.C.), most of them had probably completed their task (Ezra 7:6, 11, 12; Nehemiah 8:8). The Jews kept the collection of Old Testament Scriptures in the tabernacle and later in the temple; God's people had recognized these books from their origin as the inspired revelation from God. The Jews divided them into three major parts: Law, Prophets, and Writings. The Lord Jesus Himself acknowledged this same collection of sacred writings as the revealed Word of God (Luke 24:27, 44).

The 27 New Testament Books

The New Testament books appeared over a period of about 70 years after Christ's death and resurrection. The writers used the Greek language exclusively. Unlike the Old Testament writers, these men wrote to and from many places. No one gathered the New Testament books into a central place, such as a temple, because there was no central place of worship. Local collections of New Testament books (or copies of them) appeared in places such as Ephesus, Corinth, and Rome.

In the fourth century, the early church had to decide which books to accept as inspired of God. Many false teachers had also written pious-sounding books; in fact, many basically sound writers had produced books which seemed authoritative to many sincere believers—books like *First* and *Second Clement, Enoch, Epistle of Barnabas, Vision of Paul, Apocalypse of Peter, Shepherd of Hermas,* and the *Teaching of the Twelve Apostles.* Of course, Peter, Paul, and other apostles did not write these spurious works, and in this critical time of severe persecution, true Christians had to decide which

King James (Authorized) Version of 1611. The apocryphal book called the Wisdom of Solomon.

books were worth dying for. Finally, at a council in Carthage in A.D. 397, these earnest believers recognized, in an "official" way, the same collection of New Testament books which true believers had for centuries acknowledged as the true canon of Scripture. Applied to the Bible, the word "canon" refers to those books which Spirit-filled and Spirit-led believers "measured" and recognized as inspired of God.

Today, we have lists of New Testament books from as early as the second century which are almost identical with our familiar 27-book list. Athanasius of Alexandria (c. 298-373) was the first to apply the term *canonical* to the exact 27 books that we have in the New Testament. Earlier men, like Origen of Alexandria (c. 185-254), had already recorded the same list.

The primitive church employed four basic "principles of canonicity" to determine which books to adopt. The first principle was the principle of "apostolicity of authorship." Using this principle the early Christians asked themselves certain questions concerning each book: "Did an apostle or a member of the 'apostolic circle' write this book?" "Was the writer closely associated with an apostle?" They asked such questions especially in regard to books like Mark, Luke, and Acts. The second principle, that of "contents," posed additional questions: "Are the book's contents on a spiritual par with the apostolic books?" "Do they agree with or do they contradict the rest of the Scriptures?" This important principle challenged the Apocrypha. The third principle was the principle of "universality," which asked, "Does the church universally acknowledge and receive this book as inspired of God?" This principle eliminated such questionable works as *First Clement* and the *Epistle of Barnabas.* The final and most important principle was the principle of "inspiration," which asked the most vital questions: "Does this book bear the internal marks of inspiration?" "Does it give evidence of being divinely inspired?" "Does it edify the saints?" "Does the voice of the Holy Spirit speak through it?" This was the ultimate test whereby every believer could know that he had every word which God had breathed as sacred Scripture.

The Scripture canon, or collection of inspired books, came from the Holy Spirit who first moved upon holy men to write it. The determining factor of canonicity was not the church's authority (or church councils), but the Holy Spirit's authority. The divinely-inspired writings alone could convey the Holy Spirit's voice to God's people. God, through His Spirit, sealed with divine authority only those books which had proceeded from Him.

Our God has not only given His Word; He has preserved it in literally thousands of manuscript copies of the Scriptures. It is amazing that there exist so few variations in the many copies and that the existing variations affect no doctrine whatsoever. The remainder of this book attempts to answer how we actually got our Bible as we have it today.

The Jerusalem Chamber

The Westminster company of King James translators used the Jerusalem Chamber of Westminster Abbey in London as their workshop. Today this room, the official reception room for the Dean of Westminster, is not open to the public. Dr. Bob Jones, Chancellor of Bob Jones University, secured permission from the Dean and the Chapter of Westminster Abbey to build a replica of it in the University's Mack Memorial Library. With the cooperation of Peter Foster, Surveyor of the Fabric of Westminster Abbey (the resident architect), careful measurements were taken to ensure that the reproduction would be faithful to the original, except for the height of the ceiling, which in the replica is early Tudor, the style of the early XVI century.

Bob Jones University's Jerusalem Chamber displays, in handsome wooden cases, a rare collection of old Bibles and original leaves or pages from famous Bibles. The pictures in this pictorial history are of documents in this collection.

NOTE: A glossary of terms used in this book appears in the back.

The Development of English Bibles

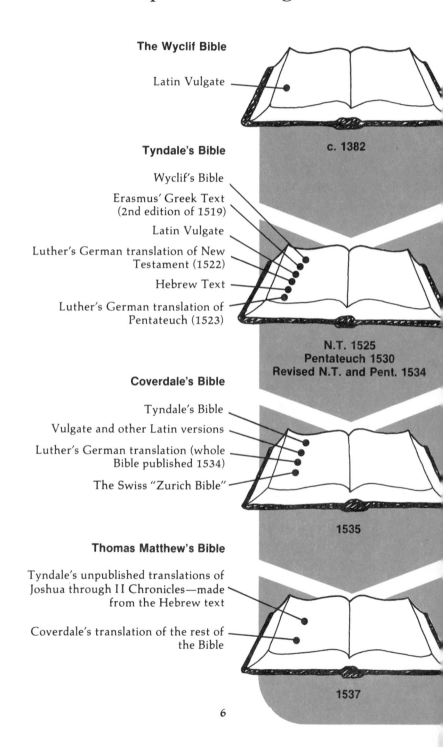

The Wyclif Bible

Latin Vulgate

c. 1382

Tyndale's Bible

Wyclif's Bible

Erasmus' Greek Text (2nd edition of 1519)

Latin Vulgate

Luther's German translation of New Testament (1522)

Hebrew Text

Luther's German translation of Pentateuch (1523)

N.T. 1525
Pentateuch 1530
Revised N.T. and Pent. 1534

Coverdale's Bible

Tyndale's Bible

Vulgate and other Latin versions

Luther's German translation (whole Bible published 1534)

The Swiss "Zurich Bible"

1535

Thomas Matthew's Bible

Tyndale's unpublished translations of Joshua through II Chronicles—made from the Hebrew text

Coverdale's translation of the rest of the Bible

1537

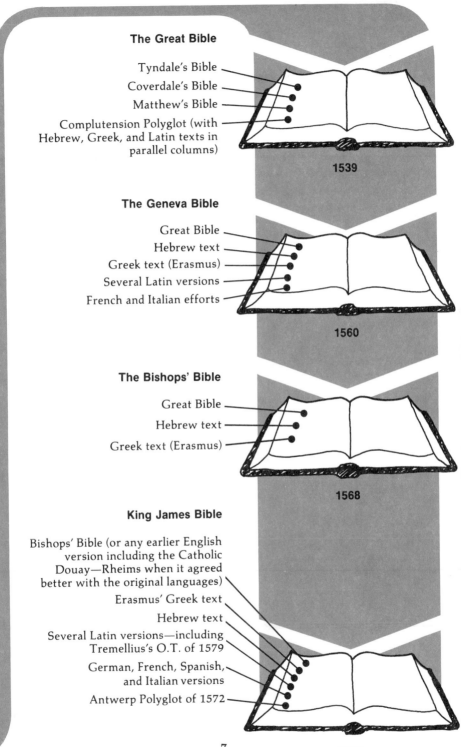

The Great Bible

Tyndale's Bible
Coverdale's Bible
Matthew's Bible
Complutension Polyglot (with Hebrew, Greek, and Latin texts in parallel columns)

1539

The Geneva Bible

Great Bible
Hebrew text
Greek text (Erasmus)
Several Latin versions
French and Italian efforts

1560

The Bishops' Bible

Great Bible
Hebrew text
Greek text (Erasmus)

1568

King James Bible

Bishops' Bible (or any earlier English version including the Catholic Douay—Rheims when it agreed better with the original languages)
Erasmus' Greek text
Hebrew text
Several Latin versions—including Tremellius's O.T. of 1579
German, French, Spanish, and Italian versions
Antwerp Polyglot of 1572

7

1611

þe euuangelie of Joon

¶ þe bygynnynge was þe worde (þat is C~ ₁~ goddis sone)/ and þe worde was at god · ɇ god was þe worde/ þis was in þe bigynnynge at god/ alle þingis ben made by hym: and wiþ outen hym is made nouȝt/ þat þing þat is made: in hym was liif/and þe liif was þe liȝte of men/and þe liȝte lcþyneþ in dirkeneffis

ɇ dirkeneffis comprehenden (or taken) not it/a man was fente fro god: to whom þe name was ioon/ þis man came into wit- neffynge · þat he fchulde bere witneffynge of þe liȝt · þat alle men fchulde bileue by hym/ he was not þe liȝt: but þat he fchulde bere witneffynge of þe liȝt · it was verrey liȝte þe whiche liȝteneþ eche man comynge into þis worlde/ he was in þe worlde · ɇ þe worlde was made by hym: and þe worlde knewe hym not/ he came into his owne þingis: and hes re- cepueden hym not/forfoþe how manye euer recepueden hym: he ȝaue to hem power for to be made þe fones of god: to hem þat bileueden in his name/ þe whiche not of bloodis · neþer of wille of fleþfche · neþer of wille of man: but ben borne of god/ and þe worde (þat is goddis fone): is made fleþfche (or man)· ɇ haþ dwellide in vs/ and we hane feen þe glorie of hym: þe glorie as of þe one bigoten of þe fadir/ þe fone ful of grace ɇ treuþe// ¶ Jon beriþ witneffynge of hym: and crieþ feyinge/ þis it was of whom J feyde/ he þat is to come aftir me · is made bifore me · for he was þe former þan J/and of þe plenty of hym: we alle hane taken ɇ grace for grace/ for þe lawe is ȝouen by moyfes: forfoþe grace ɇ treuþe is made by þu crift/ no man euer fiȝe god · no but þe one bigoten fone þat is in þe bofum of þe fadir: he haþ tolde oute/and þis is þe witneffynge of

The Wyclif Bible. Translated about 1384, became the most-loved and most-hated book of the fifteenth century. John Wyclif provided the initiative and leadership for the production of this "first English Bible," but the Roman Catholic church pronounced him a heretic and placed his Bible under the ban. No one printed Wyclif's version until the middle of the nineteenth century. This copy, dated 1848, is one of the earliest printed copies. It is opened here to John's Gospel, chapter one.

The Wyclif Bible

John Wyclif (c. 1320-1384)—English patriot, brilliant scholar, Bible preacher, wise counselor, prolific writer, popular lecturer, and forerunner of the Reformation— fully earned the familiar epithet, "morning star of the Reformation." Wyclif lived when papal prestige was at its lowest. An important influence on his views of papal authority was the "Babylonian Captivity" of the church, a time when the popes, largely under the control of French kings, maintained their residence at Avignon, France, from 1309 to 1378. Following this was the Great Schism, when for nearly 40 years (1378-1414) there were two, sometimes three, popes—some at Avignon, some at Rome—competing for recognition and power.

England herself was suffering great unrest, economic depression, and widespread tension. The so-called Hundred Years' War (1337-1453) between England and France was still flaring, and the French papacy had done little to enhance the authority of the church in the eyes of many loyal Englishmen, including John Wyclif. Finding loyal support and protection in John of Gaunt, a son of King Edward III, Wyclif advocated that the civil government should rid itself of the immoral clergymen occupying many of the great offices of state.

With many of the nobility already reading French Bibles, Wyclif believed that if the common people had the Bible in their own language they would demand a reformation of the church. The national honor of England seemed to demand a purging, and only an English Bible could work such a purging. Although the Roman Catholic church, at a council held in Toulouse, France, in 1229, had forbidden the use of the Bible to laymen, Wyclif stood forth as the champion of an open Bible. Many of his traveling preachers, called Lollards, were laymen. Some, like Wyclif, were Oxford scholars. These "pore priests" cried out against the corruption and laxity in the church. When the ministers of the apostate Roman church failed to silence these "Bible men," they used a tactic which has often worked—they falsely identified good men with radicalism and extremism.

At that time many peasants, often under the leadership of self-seeking opportunists, were revolting against England's civil laws and authorities. The most notorious of these uprisings was the Wat Tyler rebellion of 1381, which resulted in the death of Simon Sudbury, the Archbishop of Canterbury. Of course, Wyclif had no more to do with these revolts than Martin Luther had to do with the peasants' revolt in Wittenberg in 1524-1525, but it became convenient to Wyclif's opponents to label such stirrings as "Lollard uprisings." Charged with heresy and driven from Oxford in 1382, Wyclif withdrew to his parish of Lutterworth. By this time, however, the great precursor of the Reformation had already determined to give England a Bible.

Wyclif knew no Hebrew and probably no Greek, but he used what he had—the Latin Vulgate. He translated directly from the Latin into the English vernacular. It is impossible to determine Wyclif's exact role in the actual work of translating, but this great man initiated its inception and encouraged its completion. Nicholas of Hereford, one of Wyclif's Oxford associates, likely translated the Old Testament and much of the Apocrypha. Then shortly after Wyclif died of a stroke in 1384, his secretary, John Purvey, revised the entire translation.

Gradually disseminated throughout England, though not without great opposition, the Wyclif Bible—the first English Bible—became simultaneously the most-loved and most-hated book of the fifteenth century. In fact, King Henry IV enacted the statute *de Haeretico Comburendo* in 1401, which made "heresy" a secular crime punishable by burning. Roman Catholic courts, greatly enhanced by such a law, tried the "heretics" by ecclesiastical canon laws and handed the convicted ones over to the secular courts for burning. The Lollards were branded as "heretics," but continued to preach and circulate the Bible.

However, the demand for the Scriptures far exceeded the supply. There were no printing presses in those days, and copyists had to prepare each Bible by hand. The price for an hour's loan of the Bible was a load of hay. Scores used it regularly for private reading lessons. The influence of the Word of God was so great that ecclesiastical opponents were crying, "The jewel of the clergy has become the toy of the laity."

Because the marginal notes and forewords in many of the manuscript copies sharply criticized the corrupt Roman church, the English bishops did what the bishops of no other country had done—they forbade the circulation of the Bible in the vernacular. A convocation held in Oxford in 1408 instituted and vigorously enforced a penalty of burning for owning or even reading the English Scriptures. No one could translate the Bible into English without a bishop's license. A Roman Catholic papal decree in 1413 banned Wyclif's books, and another law, in 1414, warned that any who should read the English Bible should "forfeite lande, catel, lif, and godes [goods], from theyre heyres [heirs] forever." Finally, the Council of Constance, in 1415, ordered Wyclif's books burned and even had his bones exhumed, a decree carried out in 1428 under Pope Martin V. The opposition apparently failed, since 170 manuscript copies of the Wyclif Bible survive to this day, and of these, about 30 belong to Wyclif's original version of around 1382. Wyclif's Bible extended its influence even to the Continent. After Anne of Bohemia went to England to become Richard II's queen, many Bohemian scholars traveled to England's universities and carried Wyclif's books back to the University of Prague, where John Hus and others like him read them. Even long after the invention of printing, however, no one would dare print this version. Many of Wyclif's eloquent expressions are ancestors of well-known phrases in the King James Version: "strait is the gate, and narowe is the way" and "the beame and the mote" are typical of the fourteenth century. Wyclif helped set the standard for English prose.

The Gutenberg Bible

Johann Gensfleisch zur Laden—best known as John Gutenberg, the son of a fifteenth-century patrician German family—received his earliest training and experience as a goldsmith and gem-cutter; he worked at the ecclesiastical mint in Mainz, Germany. In 1434 he moved to Strasbourg and began to experiment secretly in the art of printing. The winepresses in the local vineyards likely served as models for Gutenberg's first press. He had learned to cut punches while working as a goldsmith. However, he encountered numerous problems in the art of type-casting and composition, which he solved only after much trial and error. Gutenberg returned to Mainz, where in about 1450 he is believed to have perfected the first movable-type printing press. His invention soon ignited flames of Renaissance learning and carried the doctrines of the Reformation throughout Europe. Between 1457 and 1500, presses appeared in such key cities as Augsburg, Cologne, Strasbourg, Nurenberg, Ulm, Basle, Rome, Venice, Florence, Paris, and Westminster. The first major book in the west to be printed from movable type print was the "Gutenberg Bible" printed in Mainz, about 1456 (the printer placed no date on his work).

Gutenberg cut 290 characters in elegant Gothic style and printed Jerome's Latin Vulgate on 1282 sheets of paper. The work bore his specially-designed imprint—the ox-head, stick, and star. Gutenberg left spaces for capital letters and headings. As each set of sheets came from the press, the printer sent them to a professional scribe, or rubricator, who inserted the titles by hand in red ink. Next, Gutenberg commissioned an artist to illuminate the pages of the text, ornamenting the margins and initial capitals with miniature biblical scenes and flowered borders. Delicately sketched flora and fauna make the pages come alive, with peacocks, storks, eagles, and

The Gutenberg Bible. The first book published on John Gutenberg's movable-type printing press, about 1456, was this Latin Bible, which Jerome had translated from the Greek and Hebrew over a thousand years earlier.

parrots chasing each other through a profusion of medieval foliage which curls and winds along the borders of the leaves. Myriads of blossoms fill the pages with artistic color. Each sheet has two columns, and each column contains 42 lines of print—thus the appellation, the "42-line Bible." Ligators stitched the sheets together in two volumes and bound them between handsomely-tooled leather covers. Thus, the contributions of painter and binder—each practicing an art rather than a craft— rendered each copy of Gutenberg's Bible unique, with a character all its own—a masterpiece in Gothic art.

The first edition of the 42-line Bible was at least six months in production; the exact number of copies printed is unknown, but most estimates say there were about 200. The entire edition was lost to the knowledge of scholars until a copy was identified as an original in 1763 in Cardinal Mazarin's library in France; for this reason, the Gutenberg Bible is often called the "Mazarin Bible." There are about 47 known copies in existence today. Although the 42-line Bible sold in Gutenberg's day for

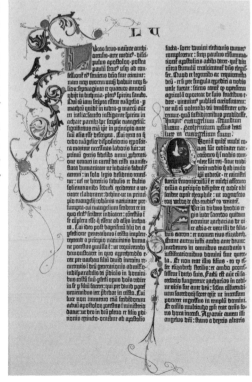

As each set of sheets came from the press, the printer sent them to a professional scribe, or rubricator, who inserted the titles by hand in red ink.

about 100 Rhenish guilders, a copy sold a few years ago at Christie's Auction for two million dollars. Another copy, in the Library of Congress, Washington, D.C., was purchased for $400,000. There is also a fine copy in the Henry E. Huntington Library in San Marino, California. Probably the most beautiful original is in the Staatsbibliothek Preussischer Kultur Besitz in Berlin.

The complete story of John Gutenberg and his printing press is unknown. He probably was not the first to use movable type printing, and he may not have completed his first edition of the Bible. Gutenberg went broke and may have been forced to turn the work over to others for completion. Johann Fust, a goldsmith from whom Gutenberg borrowed a substantial amount of money, took the printer to court in 1455 to collect the delinquent debt. Peter Schoeffer, one of Gutenberg's employees, testified in behalf of Fust, and a printing partnership was soon established between Fust and Schoeffer. These two men became the prominent printers of Mainz who produced the magnificent Psalter in 1457—the first printed work that was dated. It is possible that Fust and Schoeffer also finished the first edition of the Bible which Gutenberg began. Most important, however, is that by 1500 most of the vernacular tongues of Europe had their own published translations of the Word of God, and the stage was set for the sixteenth-century Reformation.

The Tyndale Bible

Many assume today that England was one of the first countries to receive the Bible in its native language, but the fact is that no portion of the English Scriptures appeared in print until after almost every European country and at least one African country had the Bible printed in their languages. The Latin Bible (1456), the German (about 1466), the Italian (1471), the Bohemian or Czech (1475 and 1488), the French (1477 and 1487), the Spanish (1478), the Portuguese (1495), the Serbian (1495), the Ethiopic (1513), the Danish and Norwegian (1515), the Arabic (1516), and the White Russian (1517) were all printed before the English Tyndale Bible. Even Luther's new German translation appeared as early as 1522. Certainly the English could have published John Wyclif's Bible, translated about 1382, but the church still regarded Wyclif as a heretic and, therefore, still banned his works. The Lollards continued to secretly read the Scriptures and to copy them by hand, but no English printer dared to publish the Bible until King Henry VIII had severed formal ties with the papacy. Even Tyndale fled to Hamburg. It was not until 1537 that an English printing of the whole Bible (the second edition of Coverdale's) appeared.

Progress in many areas marked the half-century following the invention of the printing press. The God of Heaven was preparing Europe for the sixteenth-century Reformation. The capture of Constantinople by the Turks in 1453 resulted in a great westward movement of Greek scholars with their manuscripts. Numerous events rapidly occurred which were to have tremendous influence upon the future translation and distribution of the Scriptures: the appearance in 1456 of the Latin Gutenberg Bible; the publication in 1457 of the first dated printed work, the Latin Psalter; the first public teaching of Greek in 1458 in the University of Paris; the publication in 1476 of the first Greek grammar; the publication in 1480 of the first Greek lexicon; and in 1488 the first printed Hebrew Bible. In 1492 (the year Columbus discovered the New World) Ferdinand and Isabella's expulsion of the Jewish population from Spain sent some 300,000 Jewish exiles all over Europe, many of them becoming teachers, some quite famous for their knowledge of Hebrew and Hebraic culture; also in 1492 (five years before Vasco da Gama rounded the Cape of Good Hope) Oxford University hired its first Greek

CHAPTER III. 16—29.] ΕΥΑΓΓΕΛΙΟΝ [THE GOSPEL

‘ μὴ ἀπόληται, ἀλλ᾽ | ἔχῃ ζωὴν αἰώνιον. ¹⁶ οὕτω γὰρ ἠγάπησεν ὁ Θεὸς τὸν κόσμον,
‘ ὥστε τὸν υἱὸν αὐτοῦ τὸν μονογενῆ ἔδωκεν, ἵνα πᾶς ὁ πιστεύων εἰς αὐτὸν μὴ
‘ ἀπόληται, ἀλλ᾽ ἔχῃ ζωὴν αἰώνιον. ¹⁷ οὐ γὰρ ἀπέστειλεν ὁ Θεὸς τὸν υἱὸν ᵃαὐτοῦ|
‘ εἰς τὸν κόσμον, ἵνα κρίνῃ τὸν κόσμον, ἀλλ᾽ ἵνα σωθῇ ὁ κόσμος δι᾽ αὐτοῦ. ¹⁸ ὁ
‘ πιστεύων εἰς αὐτὸν οὐ κρίνεται· ὁ δὲ μὴ πιστεύων ἤδη κέκριται, ὅτι μὴ πεπί-
‘ στευκεν εἰς τὸ ὄνομα τοῦ μονογενοῦς υἱοῦ τοῦ Θεοῦ. ¹⁹ αὕτη δέ ἐστιν ἡ κρίσις,
‘ ὅτι τὸ φῶς ἐλήλυθεν εἰς τὸν κόσμον, καὶ ἠγάπησαν οἱ ἄνθρωποι μᾶλλον τὸ σκότος,
‘ ἢ τὸ φῶς· ἦν γὰρ ᵇπονηρὰ αὐτῶν| τὰ ἔργα. ²⁰ πᾶς γὰρ ὁ φαῦλα πράσσων, μισεῖ
‘ τὸ φῶς, καὶ οὐκ ἔρχεται πρὸς τὸ φῶς, ἵνα μὴ ἐλεγχθῇ τὰ ἔργα αὐτοῦ· ²¹ ὁ δὲ
‘ ποιῶν τὴν ἀλήθειαν, ἔρχεται πρὸς τὸ φῶς, ἵνα φανερωθῇ αὐτοῦ τὰ ἔργα, ὅτι ἐν
‘ Θεῷ ἐστιν εἰργασμένα.’

ᵃ Alex. = μὴ ἀπόληται, ἀλλ᾽.   ᵇ Alex. = αὐτοῦ.

WICLIF — 1380	TYNDALE — 1534	CRANMER — 1539
hym perisch not but haue euerlastynge lijf.	in him perisshe : but haue eternall lyfe. For God so loueth the worlde: that he hath geven his only sonne, ¹⁶ that none	beleueth in him, perisshe not, but haue eternall lyfe.
¹⁶ for god loued so the world : that he jaf his oon bigoten sone; that eche man that bileueth in him perisch not : but haue euerlastynge liif; ¹⁷ for god sente not his sone in to the world, that he iuge the world, but that the world be sauyd bi him; ¹⁸ he that bileueth in hym, is not demyd; but he that bileueth not, is now demyd bi that he bileueth not in the name of the oon bigetun sone of god; ¹⁹ and this is the dome; for lijt cam in to the world: and men loueden more derknesse thanne lijt; for her werkis weren yuel; ²⁰ for eche man that doith yuel, hatith the lijt; and he cometh not to the lijt : that his werkis be not repreued. ²¹ but he that	that beleve in him should perisshe : but should have everlastinge lyfe. ¹⁷ For God sent not his sonne into the worlde; to condempne the worlde : but that the worlde through him might be saved. ¹⁸ He that beleveth on him; shall not be condempned. But he that beleveth not; is condempned all redy; be cause he beleveth not in the name of the only sonne of God. ¹⁹ And this is the condempnacion : that light is come into the worlde; and the men loved darcknes more then light; be-cause their dedes were evill. ²⁰ For every man that evyll doeth; hateth the light : nether commeth to light; lest his dedes should be reproved. ²¹ But he that	¹⁷ For God so loued the worlde, that he gaue his only begotten sonne, that who-soeuer beleueth in him, shulde not perisshe, but haue euerlasting lyfe. ¹⁸ For God sent not his sonne into the worlde, to condempne the worlde but that the world through him myght be saued. ¹⁹ He that beleueth on him, is not condemned. But he that beleueth not, is condemned all-redy, because he hath not beleued in the name of the onely begotten sonne of God. ²⁰ And thys is the condempnacion that lyght is come into the worlde, and men loued darckenes more then lyght, because their dedes were euyll. ²¹ For euery one

English Hexapla. John 3:16-21 from the Wyclif Bible of 1380, the Tyndale Bible of 1534, and the Cranmer (Great) Bible of 1539. The Greek text appears above.

teacher—Grocyn. In 1506, the first Hebrew lexicon appeared; in 1516 Desiderius Erasmus' Greek New Testament made its debut; and in 1517 (the year in which Luther nailed his 95 theses to the door of the Castle Church in Wittenberg, Germany) the Complutensian Polyglot Bible, with Hebrew, Greek, and Latin texts in parallel columns, appeared. Facts, however, are dull without interpretation, and the interpretation of all this is expressed in a word—"progress." The Lord God was setting the stage for the rediscovery of the great doctrines of grace. Widespread interest in the rediscovered classics prevailed. Tools for unlocking knowledge of the Hebrew and Greek Scriptures were becoming available. The authority of the Word of Life soon superceded the authority of a blind apostate church which for centuries had specialized in keeping the people in ignorance and superstition.

William Tyndale (c. 1494-1536)—born about 100 years after John Wyclif's death—early distinguished himself both at Oxford and at Cambridge as a scholar. Although relatively few details of his life are available, it is certain that early in life Tyndale accepted the great doctrines of the Reformation. Devoted to the study of the Scriptures and full of the reforming spirit, Tyndale once remarked to a critic, "If God spare my life, ere many years I will cause the boy that driveth the plough in England to know more of the Scriptures than thou doest." About 1523 an alderman and merchant named Humphrey Monmouth hospitably received Tyndale into his London home for about a year and financially aided him in the work of translation. Monmouth wrote that Tyndale "studied most part of the day and of the night at his book." The prohibition of English translations, however, caused Tyndale to leave his homeland in 1524, never to see it again; his friend Monmouth was imprisoned in the Tower of London for giving him aid. Tyndale himself fled to Germany, where he visited Martin Luther at Wittenberg.

In Germany, Tyndale, translating from Erasmus' Greek text, completed his English New Testament and presented it to Peter Quentel, a Cologne printer, for the publication of 3000 copies in a small quarto edition which friends could easily smuggle into England. Immediately, satanic opposition arose. Soon after the work began, German Catholics overheard the Cologne printers bragging that England would soon become "Lutheran." The controversial Roman Catholic priest, John Dobneck (Cochlaeus), informed the Senate of Cologne, as well as King Henry VIII of England. Providentially learning that the Cologne Senate had ordered an imminent seizure, Tyndale and his faithful assistant William Roye hastened to the printers and escaped with the precious sheets. They made their way up the Rhine by boat to the city of Worms, where in 1525 Tyndale supervised the surreptitious publishing of his New Testament. Within a year, friends were smuggling the small, octavo-size copies into England in cases of merchandise.

Ecclesiastical authorities bought them and burned them, but Tyndale simply used the much-needed money to print more Bibles—some even in quarto size. The God of Heaven made the wrath of man to praise Him. An old English chronicler named Edward Halle relates that the

Bishop of London, Cuthbert Tunstall (or Tonstall), thought he "had God by the toe, when indeed he had the devil by the fist." The bishops, preferring to use the Romish term *do penance,* rejected Tyndale's word *repent.* Even Sir Thomas More, who was later beheaded because of his opposition to Henry VIII's divorce, greatly criticized Tyndale's translation, charging it with many gross errors. A brief look at England's political climate is indispensable for a proper understanding of the history of the English Bible.

King Henry VIII, distressed about the inability of his wife, Catherine of Aragon, to bear him a male successor, tried to obtain sanction from Pope Clement VII to divorce Catherine and to marry her maid of honor, Anne Boleyn. Catherine had been the widow of Henry's elder brother, and a previous pope had granted a special "dispensation" for Henry to marry her. With his application for an annulment of this marriage, Henry argued from the Bible that "if a man shall take his brother's wife, it is an unclean thing: he hath uncovered his brother's nakedness; they shall be childless" (Leviticus 20:21). Although Pope Clement VII was quite fond of Henry, he found himself in a very awkward position—he was virtually a prisoner of war to Catherine's nephew, Emperor Charles V. Proceeding to Rome in 1527, Charles' Spanish troops had stormed and looted the city and had nearly made the pope a prisoner in his own Castle of St. Angelo. Determined, therefore, to remove his kingdom from the jurisdiction of the Roman papacy, Henry VIII, by the Act of Supremacy in 1534, became the "Supreme Head" of the Church of England. Thomas Cranmer, Archbishop of Canterbury, pronounced Henry's marriage void and Catherine's daughter Mary illegitimate. Only a few days before Cranmer's decision, Henry had married Anne Boleyn, who was already pregnant (with Elizabeth). In the same year (1534), the Upper House (Bishops) of Convocation of Cambridge petitioned the Crown to authorize a translation of the Bible into English, and although no immediate results came of this, it became obvious that England's political climate was now changing in favor of an English Bible.

William Tyndale, meanwhile, had diligently studied Hebrew, translated the entire Pentateuch and the book of Jonah (with many marginal notes), and published them in 1530-1531. Then, in 1534, using the second and third editions of Erasmus' Greek text and Wyclif's and Luther's translations, Tyndale published, at Antwerp, a timely new revision of his Pentateuch and New Testament and presented a beautiful copy to Queen Anne. This copy is still preserved in the British Museum. This 1534 revision became the standard for all future revisions of the English Bible, including the King James Version of 1611. The English-speaking world, however, did not immediately accept Tyndale's Bible. The editor's notes in the 1534 edition clearly reveal the reason—Luther's influence. Even after the break with the papacy, Henry VIII still considered himself an orthodox Catholic and offered no support to or even sympathy with Tyndale and his Bible. The general malice for Tyndale remained unabated.

Tyndale went to Antwerp, a "free city" in 1535, where he was allowed political asylum to continue his work unmolested. But one of his own countrymen, Henry Philips, viciously betrayed him. Tyndale had accepted Philips into his circle of friends and actually loaned him 40 shillings on the morning of his betrayal. Charles V controlled the territory surrounding Antwerp and on May 31, 1535, Philips, a rabid Roman Catholic, lured Tyndale some distance from his dwelling, where Charles' officers treacherously seized him. They conveyed Tyndale out of Antwerp and imprisoned him in the dungeon of Vilvorde Castle, a fortress some six miles north of Brussels, where he remained until October, 1536. From that cell, Tyndale penned a sad letter appealing for a warmer cap: "I suffer extremely from cold in the head, being afflicted with a perpetual catarrh, which is considerably increased in the cell; also a piece of cloth, to patch my leggings. My overcoat has been worn out. My shirts also are worn out. I also wish his [the jailer's] permission to have a candle in the evening; for it is wearisome to sit alone in the dark. But above all things, I entreat and beseech your clemency to be urgent with the Procureur, that he may kindly suffer me to have my Hebrew Bible, Grammar, and Dictionary, that I may spend my time with that study."

Tyndale's request was probably granted, and it is likely that in that prison cell he translated Joshua through II Chronicles and passed the manuscripts on to John Rogers, who definitely incorporated them into the Matthew Bible after Tyndale's death.

The Roman Catholic church found William Tyndale guilty of heresy and handed him over to the secular powers for execution. On October 6, 1536, governmental authorities led him to the stake and strangled and burned him in the prison yard. In a loud voice, his dying words rang out, "Lord, open the King of England's eyes." God answered the martyr's prayer. Even before Tyndale's death, German printers had published the Coverdale Bible—the first complete Bible translated into English—based largely upon Tyndale's work. Moreover, various publishers disseminated approximately 50,000 copies of Tyndale's own Bible before his death.

William Tyndale's translations of the New Testament and a large part of the Old Testament not only form the basis, in phrasing, vocabulary, and musical rhythm, for the same books in the King James Bible (1611), but actually constitute over four-fifths of the King James translation. All that remains today of Tyndale's New Testament are three fragments—one quarto and two octavo editions. Housed in the British Museum, the quarto consists of some 60 pages including eight of the actual sheets printed in Cologne before Tyndale was forced to flee with the sheets to Worms. An octavo edition, with only its title page missing, is now at the Baptist College, Bristol, England. The other octavo edition, an imperfect one, is in the library of St. Paul's Cathedral in London. The octavo-size Bible originally sold at Worms in Tyndale's day for half a crown a copy—five full days' wages for a mason. Dutch printers sold the octavo for 13 pence.

Tyndale's rendering of John 10:16 is more accurate than most of the early English versions: "and other shepe I have, which are not of this folde. Them also must I bringe, that they maye heare my voyce, and that ther maye be one *flocke* [even the King James wrongly has it "fold"] and one sherpeherde." Tyndale did give some renderings which sound a bit amusing to the modern reader; for example at Genesis 39:2, he has it, "And the Lord was with Joseph, and he was a lucky fellow." The serpent says to Eve in Genesis 3:4, "Tush, ye shall not die." Finally, Tyndale's marginal note of warning at Exodus 32:15 (the golden calf incident) reveals his hatred of error and his love for truth: "The Pope's bull slayeth more than Aaron's calf."

The Coverdale Bible

Miles Coverdale (1488-1569) believed in the great biblical principles and ideas of the Reformation. Like Tyndale, he too had to flee from England to the Continent in about 1528, where he possibly assisted William Tyndale in Hamburg and began his own work of translating the Bible into English. The Coverdale Bible—the first complete English Bible ever printed—appeared in 1535, published in six folio volumes at either Marburg or Cologne. On the title page, Coverdale claims to have "translated out of Douche [German] and Latyn into Englishe." Coverdale did not know Greek and Hebrew; he was deeply indebted to Luther's German translation, to the Latin Vulgate, and especially to Tyndale's version. He also relied upon a Swiss version, but with only minor revisions, he used Tyndale's New Testament and those Old Testament books which Tyndale had rendered into English. Coverdale possessed a

The Coverdale Bible. First complete English Bible ever printed. Miles Coverdale based this translation largely upon William Tyndale's and Martin Luther's versions and published it in 1535. This is an original leaf from the book of Job.

beautiful literary style and a delicate ear for cadence. His rendering of the Psalms still forms part of the *Book of Common Prayer*. On the dedicatory page of his Bible, the translator says that he has "nether wrested nor altered so much as one worde for the maytenaunce of any maner of secte: but haue with a cleare conscience purely and faythfully translated this out of fyue sundry interpreters, hauying onely the manyfest trueth of the scripture before myne eyes."

Although Coverdale published his first edition on the Continent, he openly dedicated it to the King of England— Henry VIII. A diplomat of no small ability, Miles Coverdale excluded the controversial notes which had made English authorities so bitterly oppose Tyndale's Bible. The title page of the Coverdale Bible depicts King Henry seated and crowned—the royal arms of England at his feet. His right hand holds a drawn sword; with his left hand, Henry dispenses the Bible to the mitred bishops. A humble dedicatory epistle praises the king as the true "defender of the faith." Further, the epistle denounces the errors of "the blind bishop of Rome." Thus, by both word and illustration, Coverdale demonstrates how the Bible could aid Henry as both the King of England and the Supreme Head of the Church of England. Thomas Cromwell, the king's Vicar General (the second man in the church, ranking even above the Archbishop of Canterbury), became a major protector of Coverdale's Bible.

Even though the general mood of England favored an English Bible, any official authorization of Tyndale's, since Henry VIII had unnecessarily sanctioned his kidnapping and martyrdom on foreign soil, would have seemed unwise. Under such sensitive circumstances, Cromwell probably feared that the king might return his obedience to the pope, especially after Henry beheaded Queen Anne on May 19, 1536, and ordered Parliament to pronounce his marriage to her void and their daughter Elizabeth illegitimate. Anne, who had received a copy of Tyndale's Bible, had also placed a copy of Coverdale's Bible in her chamber.

The second edition of Coverdale's Bible (a big folio edition) became, in 1537, the first complete English Bible printed in England. Henry VIII himself licensed it. Many have referred to it as the "Bug Bible" for its rendering of Psalm 91:5: "Thou shalt not nede to be afrayed for any *bugges* by night." This is not a unique use of the word *bug*, however, because Wyclif had used it in his translation of Baruch 6:69; even the Matthew Bible uses the word. Bug carried the idea of "bugaboo" or "bogey" (an imaginary object of fear); thus, in Shakespeare's *Henry VI*, Warwick ironically was the "*bugge* that feared us all." Another interesting translation in the Coverdale Bible is its rendering of Judges 15:19, "Then God opened a gome tooth in the cheke bone so the water went out," and in I Kings 22:34, a man "shott the king of Israel between the mawe and the lungs." Coverdale's Bible was the first to introduce chapter summaries, as distinct from simple chapter headings.

The Matthew Bible. John Rogers published this version in 1537 under the pseudonym, "Thomas Matthew." It was largely William Tyndale's translation, but Tyndale's name was in such disfavor with the king that no publisher would use it. This leaf is from a 1549 edition and shows sections from Zechariah 1-4.

The Matthew Bible

Just before his death, Tyndale had given to his friend

John Rogers, who was chaplain to the English Merchant Adventurers at Antwerp, the hand-written manuscripts of his Old Testament translations of the books of Joshua through II Chronicles. Rogers substituted Tyndale's translations of these books—made from the Hebrew—for those of Coverdale—made from the English, Latin, and German. Slightly revising the other books of the Coverdale Bible and adding some marginal notes, John Rogers published the new version in Antwerp in 1537 under the pseudonym, "Thomas Matthew."

Many woodcuts embellish both the Old and New Testaments, the book of Revelation having one to each chapter. Although the complete work was largely Tyndale's translation, Tyndale's name was in such disfavor with the king that Rogers withheld it. Cromwell and Thomas Cranmer, however, procured for the "Matthew Bible" a license from the king, who did not realize Tyndale's contribution to it. Thus, the very work for which William Tyndale had died now became, along with the Coverdale Bible, officially licensed by the king, whose eyes Tyndale had so sacrificially "prayed open." Again, the Lord God made the wrath of man to praise Him. "The King's heart is in the hand of the Lord, as the rivers of water: he turneth it whithersoever he will" (Proverbs 21:1). The official license meant that these Bibles could be privately owned and read, bought and sold, without interference from the authorities.

The Matthew Bible contains about 2000 marginal notes, one of which gave this Bible the title "Wife-Beating Bible." The note at I Peter 3, where the Apostle instructs husbands how to treat their wives, explains that "if she be not obedient and healpfull unto hym [he] endeavoureth to beate the feare of God into her heade, that therby she maye be compelled to learne her dutie, and to do it." Like Coverdale's Bible, the Matthew Bible places the Apocrypha in an appendix to the Old Testament. Richard Taverner in 1539 issued a slightly-edited reprint of the Matthew Bible.

The.xiiii.Chapter.

The Lord denieth his worde to the people for their synnes sake. The despysers of the worde doth the Lorde sometyme deceaue by false prophetes. A comforte of them that fled unto Babylon.

There resorted * unto me certayne of the elders of Israell, and sate downe by me. Then came the worde of the Lorde vnto me, sayinge: thou sonne of man, these me beare theyr vnclenes in their hertes, & go purposely vpon the stombling blocke of theyr owne wyckednesse: shoulde I then answere at theyr requeste? Therfore speake vnto them, and saye: thus sayeth the Lorde God: Euery man of the house of Israell, that beareth hys vncleane Idolles in hys herte, purposynge to stomble in hys owne wyckednes, and commeth to a prophet, to enquyre any thyng at me by hym: vnto that man wyl I the Lord my selfe giue answere, accordyng to the multitude of hys Idolles: that the house of Israell maye be snared in theyr owne hertes, becaufe they be cleane gone from me, for theyr abbominacions sakes. Wherfore, tel ȳ house of Israel: thus sayeth the Lorde God: *Be conuerted, for sake your Idolles, and turne your wyttes from your fylthynesse, and turne your faces from all youre abhominacions.

For euery man, (whether he be of the house

Ezec. 20. 8

2

33

Esa. 10. e

The Great Bible. Prepared by Miles Coverdale and published in 1539, this is a revision of the Matthew Bible. Many people heard the Word of God for the first time as their ministers read from the Great Bible, which was chained to the churches' reading desks. This page contains a portion of Ezekiel 13.

The Great Bible

In 1538 Thomas Cromwell, the King's Vicar General, entrusted to Miles Coverdale the work of revising the Matthew Bible, striking out the controversial marginal notes. Cromwell then sent the new revision to Paris, whose printers were known for their magnificent work. However, the French Inquisitor-General raided the print shop and confiscated some 2500 Bibles which were in the final stages of completion. Some believe that Cromwell's men recovered these Bibles. Coverdale and his associates did succeed in conveying the type and printing equipment to London, where King Henry VIII had just received word of his excommunication by the pope.

In 1539, the "Great Bible" was published. It was so-called for its physical dimensions of 16½" x 11". Even on its title page it had political propaganda, discernible even to the most illiterate who flocked to the churches to see this great volume chained to the sacred reading desks. On its frontispiece—said to be designed by the eminent German painter, Hans Holbein the Younger (1497-1543), who resided in England after 1536—the Great Bible depicts the king, a benevolent-appearing man, handing out Bibles to Archbishop Cranmer, who distributes them to the bishops and clergy. With his left hand, King Henry hands Bibles to Thomas Cromwell, Secretary of State, who gives them to the courtiers, noblemen, and other laymen. Below this, there appears in the engraving a preacher addressing the enthusiastic common people, some of whom are shouting, "God save the Kynge!" Others express gratitude by exclaiming, *vivat rex*—"long live the King." Below at the right, some ill-favored fellows, not in harmony with Henry or with the new spirit of the times, peer out of the window bars of Newgate prison. "In God's name," proclaimed Henry VIII, "let it [the Bible] go abroad among our people."

The Great Bible, the first Bible to be specifically authorized for *public* use in English churches, provided tremendous incentive for thousands of commoners to learn to read. How frustrating it must have been to finally have a copy of the controversial book in one's own church and not be able to read it. Cromwell ordered every parson to obtain a copy and to chain it up in some convenient place in his church, in order that the parishioners might "resort to the same and read it." Only three years after the martyrdom of William Tyndale, who had promised the ploughboy of England a knowledge of the Scriptures, hundreds listened to the reading of God's Holy Word. Many lay groups hired clergymen to teach them to read, so that they could know the Scriptures. Interestingly, the Great Bible was Tyndale's work; it was a simple revision of the Matthew Bible, which was only a slight revision of Tyndale's. The official price of an unbound copy of the Great Bible was ten shillings; bound copies sold for twelve shillings. The first edition was sometimes called "Cromwell's Bible."

Thomas Cromwell's character, however, was not always exemplary. Moving in the "convenient" stream of sixteenth-century Machiavellian pragmatism, Cromwell often acted too swiftly, plundering the treasures of the monasteries and rashly destroying shrines, images, and other Catholic properties. Henry VIII, although at times a nominal supporter of the Reformation, felt that Cromwell was drawing him into an undesirable alliance with the continental reformers, thus alienating England's loyal Catholic population. Cromwell was condemned without trial for alleged bribery to prevent justice; he was executed in July 1540, and even Thomas Cranmer favored the execution. It is not surprising that with Cromwell's fall, Coverdale's revision of the Great Bible appeared with a new frontispiece. Ironically, the new title page depicts Cuthbert Tonstall, the former bishop of London who had bought up Tyndale's New Testaments to burn them at St. Paul's Cross, now supporting the new translation—a translation that was virtually Tyndale's own production.

Because of Cromwell's undiplomatic actions, the religious sentiment in England was reversing itself; so complete was this reversal that Parliament, in 1543, banned "the crafty, false, and untrue translation of Tyndale." Again, in 1546 Parliament ordained that "no man or woman . . . was to receive, have, take, or keep, Tyndale's or Coverdale's New Testament." These bans on the Bible were apparently empty formalities, for the Great Bible continued to maintain its prominent position in practically every church of the land. Thanks to the God of all true wisdom, when King Henry died on January 28, 1547, the Great Bible was still the version "appointed to the use of the churches." By this time, at least eight editions had appeared.

Henry VIII's son by the Protestant Jane Seymour, Edward VI, came to the throne at the age of nine. Having received a Protestant education, the lad appeared to many as the "new Josiah" coming to "purify the temple." During Edward's short reign of six and a half years, the New Testament underwent 24 printings and the entire Bible 16, some in quarto and some in handy octavo size, for both church and home use.

The Great Bible earned its title by its spiritual, as well as its physical, dimensions. The Psalms (Psalter) of the *Book of Common Prayer* preserve the translation of the second (1540) edition sometimes called "Cranmer's Bible," because he wrote its preface. The translation, like all other translations, has imperfections, but generally it was a good translation, and the Lord greatly used it to open scores of blind eyes to see the wonderful grace of God. The vellum pre-publication copy of the first Great Bible—now at St. John's College, Cambridge—may have been Thomas Cromwell's personal copy.

The Geneva Bible

In 1553 King Edward VI's half-sister, Mary, succeeded him to the English throne and restored papal authority in England. "Bloody Mary" prohibited the reading of the English Bible, and in 1554-1555 she burned at the stake the Protestant bishops Hugh Latimer, Nicholas Ridley, and John Hooper. Hooper is often called the "father of Puritanism." In 1556 Mary proceeded to burn Thomas Cranmer at the stake. This execution was followed by 300 others, led by the great protomartyr, John Rogers—editor of the Matthew Bible.

At the beginning of Mary's reign, approximately 800 Protestants left England. The most learned of these exiles went to Geneva, the "holy city of the Alps," which had become a sanctuary for such spiritual giants as William

Gilbey, Thomas Sampson, Theodore Beza, John Calvin, Calvin's brother-in-law William Whittingham, and John Knox (who described the Swiss city as "the most perfect school of Christ since the days of the Apostles"). Even Miles Coverdale—then 70 years of age—lived in Geneva in 1558, and he no doubt had a guiding hand in the refugees' new translation. Help also came from the French scholars at Geneva who were already working on a new revised French Bible that was to become the official translation of the Reformed Church of France. Published on April 10, 1560, and indebted partly to Tyndale's original translation and partly to the Great Bible, the Geneva Bible was the first English version to be translated entirely from the original languages.

The translators dedicated the new Bible to Queen Elizabeth, who ascended the English throne on November 17, 1558. They promised her the Puritans' loyal support. Elizabeth, however, inclined herself towards the Puritans only when it suited her political purposes. She desired foremost to make the Church of England as easy for *all* her subjects to adhere to as possible; the criterion for religious freedom was strict obedience to its "Supreme Governor," the Queen. But Elizabeth's policy was always moderate; she acted very cautiously, and her Puritan subjects usually did the same. Consequently, even though Elizabeth often discouraged the printing of the new Bibles, she did not prevent the printing of two editions of the Great Bible early in her reign, and she never opposed the importation of the Geneva Bibles during her reign.

The Geneva Bible was a grand success. The handy quarto-size volume was easier to handle than previous standard Bibles. The plain Roman type, rather than the old Gothic letters, made it more legible. What a welcome improvement! Even though the printing press had fostered a great demand for spectacles, which were readily available (especially in Germany), the optical profession was still in infancy.

The Geneva Bible was the first English version to have

43 And he charged them ſtraitly that no man ſhould knowe of it, and commaunded to giue her meate.

CHAP. VI.

2 *Chriſt preaching in his cowntrey, his owne outeeme him.* 6 *The vnbeliefe of the Nazarites.* 7 *The Apoſtles are ſent.* 13 *They caſt out deuils: they anoynt the ſicke with oyle.* 14 *Herodes opinion of Chriſt.* 18 *The cauſe of Iohns impriſonment.* 22 *Dauncing.* 27 *Iohn beheaded,* 29 *Buried.* 30 *The Apoſtles returne from preaching.* 34 *Chriſt teacheth in the deſert.* 37 *Hee feedeth the people with fiue loaues.* 48 *The Apoſtles are troubled on the ſea.* 56 *The ſicke that touch Chriſtes garment, are healed.*

A Nd ✚ 1 he departed thence, and came into his owne countrey, and his diſciples followed him.

2 And when the Sabbath was come, he began to teach in the Synagogue, and many that heard him, were aſtonied, and ſayd, From whence hath this man theſe things? and what wiſedome is this that is giuen vnto him, that euen ſuch a great works are done by his hands?

3 Is not this that carpenter Maries ſonne, the brother of Iames and Ioſes, and of Iuda and Simon? and are not his b ſiſters here with vs? And they were offended in him.

4 Then Ieſus ſaid vnto them, A ✚ Prophet is not without c honour, but in his owne countrey, and among his owne kinred, and in his owne houſe.

5 And hee d could there doe no great works, ſaue that he laid his hands vpon a few ſicke folke, and healed them.

6 And hee marueiled at their vnbelife, and went about by the townes on euery ſide, teaching.

7 ¶ x 2 And hee called vnto him the twelue, and began to ſend them foorth two and two, and gaue them power ouer vncleane ſpirits,

8 3 And commaunded them that they ſhould take nothing for their iourney, ſaue a ſtaffe onely: neither ſcrip, neither bread, neither monie in their girdles:

9 But that they ſhould be ſhod with ✚ e ſandals, and that they ſhould not put on f two coats.

10 And hee ſayd vnto them, Whereſoeuer yee ſhall enter into an houſe, g there abide till ye depart thence.

11 *4 And whoſoeuer ſhall not receiue you,

16 ✚ So when Herod heard, he ſaid, It is Iohn whom 1 I beheaded: he is riſen from the dead.

17 For Herod himſelfe had ſent forth, and had taken Iohn, & bound him in priſon for Herodias ſake, which was his brother Philips wife, becauſe he had married her.

18 For Iohn ſaid vnto Herod, ✚ It is not lawfull for thee to haue thy brothers wife.

19 Therfore Herodias m laid wait againſt him, and would haue killed him, but ſhe could not:

20 For Herod feared Iohn, knowing that he was a iuſt man, and an holy, and reuerenced him, and when he heard him, he did many things, and heard him n gladly.

21 But the time being conuenient, when Herod on his birthday made a banket to his princes and captaines, and chiefe eſtates of Galile:

22 And the daughter o of the ſame Herodias came in, and danced, and pleaſed Herod, and them that ſate at table together, the King ſaid vnto the maid, Aske of me what thou wilt, and I will giue it thee.

23 And hee ſware vnto her, Whatſoeuer thou ſhalt aske of me, I will giue it thee, euen vnto the halfe of my kingdome.

24 v So P ſhe went foorth, and ſaid to her mother, What ſhall I aske? And ſhe ſaid, Iohn Baptiſts head.

25 Then ſhee came in ſtraightway with haſte vnto the King, and asked, ſaying, I would that thou ſhouldeſt giue mee euen now in a charger the head of Iohn Baptiſt.

26 Then the King was very ſory: yet for his othes ſake, and for their ſakes which ſate at table with him, he would not refuſe her.

27 And immediatly the King ſent the q hangman, and gaue charge that his head ſhould bee brought in. So he went and beheaded him in the priſon,

28 And brought his head in a charger, and gaue it to the maide, and the maide gaue it to her mother.

29 And when his diſciples heard it, they came and tooke vp his body, and put in a tombe.

30 ¶ x And the Apoſtles gathered themſelues together to Ieſus, and tolde him all things, both what they had done, and what they had taught.

The Geneva Bible. English scholars who fled to Geneva, Switzerland, during "Bloody Mary's" persecution translated this version and published it in 1560. Shown here is a 1608 edition, opened to Mark 6—the account of John the Baptist's death. Referring to verses 21 and 22, the godly Puritan translators labeled the page "The Inconvenience of dancing."

numbered verses. Chapter divisions, as we know them, were devised three and a half centuries earlier by Stephen Langton, the thirteenth-century doctor, cardinal, and Archbishop of Canterbury. Verse divisions appeared much later: Rabbi Nathan, in 1448, invented the Old Testament verse divisions; about 1555, Robert Estienne (Stephanus or Stephens) of Paris issued a Bible, using Nathan's Old Testament divisions and his own New Testament divisions. The later English versions, beginning with the

Geneva Bible of 1560 (first published by Rowland Hall) adopted the Nathan-Estienne system. The new verse divisions, with each verse printed as though it were a new paragraph, enabled the poorly educated to master small individual units of the text.

Numerous additional innovations contributed to the Geneva Bible's rapid popularity. It was the first translation to employ the use of italics to indicate words not in the original. A brief concordance, a chronology, extensive prologues, and marginal notes explaining ancient customs added even more to the usefulness of the work. A curious feature in the Geneva Bible was the attempt to transliterate Hebrew proper names into English rather than use the common English forms—for example, *Heuah* for Eve, and *Izhak* for Isaac. A special table provided a listing of the Hebrew names with their English counterparts. Thousands of English parents named their children from this table of Bible characters instead of using the names of the "saints" on the old Roman calendar, thus influencing the nation a step further away from Romanism. The Geneva Bible also reduced the values of ancient coins to pounds sterling and gave distances between Bible locations in English statute miles. Five Bible maps and 26 engravings illustrated the new translation. Unlike earlier English Bibles, which depicted Bible characters in sixteenth-century garb, the Geneva Bible represented them, as accurately as possible, in costumes of their own period. A 1578 edition included a Bible dictionary, and some editions had the whole book of Psalms in English meter in an appendix, "with apt notes to sing them withall." Both translators and publishers agreed to relegate the Apocrypha to an Old Testament appendix.

The Scottish edition of the Geneva Bible, published in 1579, so nurtured the Scottish Reformation that the authorities totally abolished papal jurisdiction from the land. Soon afterwards, an act of Parliament authorized the Geneva Bible as the official Bible of Scotland.

God moved similarly in England, making a native

publication of the Geneva Bible inevitable. In 1570 Pope Pius V excommunicated Queen Elizabeth, who then adopted a more tolerant attitude toward the Puritans. Three years later, Elizabeth appointed Sir Thomas Walsingham, a former refugee from "Bloody Mary's" reign and still an active Puritan, as her Secretary of State. He immediately became one of the most powerful men in England. Christopher Barker, one of Walsingham's friends, purchased (probably with Walsingham's aid) from the Privy Council the right to print the Geneva Bible. Barker published in 1575 (15 years after the first Geneva publication) an attractive octavo edition—the first Geneva Bible printed in England. The frontispiece of the new edition bore the royal arms and the arms and crest of Walsingham.

In 1577 Barker made what some called "a desperate adventure": he purchased, for "a great sum," the office of "Printer to the Queen's Most Excellent Majesty." This office conferred on Barker the right to print the Bible and the *Book of Common Prayer*. Barker knew that the one book which could bring a return on his investment was the Bible. He bound the Geneva Bible with the *Book of Common Prayer* and included the Sternhold and Hopkins metrical version of the Psalms; over each musical note, he placed the proper letter indicating the tone (as "d" for "do" and "r" for "re"), thus aiding and enhancing the work of generations of musicians who taught Psalm singing. The Geneva Bible rapidly became a best-seller. Barker even made the more expensive editions available on the "installment-plan." By 1603, the year of Elizabeth's death, Christopher Barker and his son Robert had published 61 editions of the Geneva Bible, nine of the Bishops' Bibles, and numerous New Testaments.

Its terse style, improved scholarship, lucid prose, and pithy notes gave the Geneva Bible wide acceptance. It became the English household Bible, the Bible of Shakespeare, and the Puritan Bible. The Pilgrims brought a Geneva Bible to the New World on the *Mayflower*.

Long after the publication of the King James Version in 1611, the Puritans remained loyal to their beloved Geneva Bible, especially when Charles I, who ascended England's throne in 1625, appointed Bishop William Laud of London, a long-time enemy of the Geneva Bible, as one of his chief advisors. Laud's alleged prohibition of the printing of the Geneva Bible in London after 1616 was one of the charges hurled against him when he was on trial for his life in 1645. The charge was probably legitimate, for in the late 1630's and early 1640's the Puritans had at least eight editions printed on the Continent and smuggled into England. To avoid detection, these editions of the Geneva Bible bore on their titles the date "1599," the name of Christopher Barker, and an imitation of one of his title-page borders.

In 1643 Oliver Cromwell published appropriate passages from the Geneva Bible for his troops. He called this selection "The Souldiers Pocket Bible: containing the most (if not all) those places contained in holy Scripture which doe shew the qualifications of his inner man, that is a fet Souldier to fight the Lord's Battels, both before the fight, in the fight, and after the fight." Approximately 50,000 copies—five distinct editions—of this biblical ammunition were reissued to the Federal soldiers in the American Civil War.

An interesting rendering occurs at Genesis 3:7—"They sewed figge tree leaves together, and made themselves breeches"—hence, the appellation "The Breeches Bible." A mistranslation (or misprint) appears at John 6:67: "Then said *Judas* to the twelve, Will ye also go away?" Less serious is the mistake which gave the 1562 edition the title, "Place-Makers Bible"; it renders Matthew 5:9, "Blessed are the place-makers." The Dort edition of the Geneva Bible became known as "the Goose Bible," because it portrayed a goose as its emblem. The King James translators apparently understood the Geneva Bible's merits, for in the prefatory address of the "Translators to the Reader," they quote exclusively from the Geneva Bible.

The Bishops' Bible. Prepared under the direction of Matthew Parker, Archbishop of Canterbury during Queen Elizabeth's reign, and published in 1568, the Bishops' Bible was used primarily by the clergy and was generally unpopular among the common people. This page shows Proverbs 21.

The Bishops' Bible

When Queen Elizabeth came to England's throne in 1558, she first revealed her basically "conservative" mood by appointing Matthew Parker as Archbishop of Canterbury. Parker had received his ordination as a Romanist in 1527 before England's break with the papacy, and the English bishops now looked favorably at the continuity of an "apostolic episcopacy," which Parker supposedly

35

represented. At the bishops' request, Parker agreed to initiate a new "official" English translation to compete with the Geneva Bible, published in 1560 and growing in popularity among the Puritans. In 1563 Parker divided the work among certain bishops and instructed them to follow the text of the Great Bible, except where it varied from the Hebrew or Greek. These translators for the most part were undistinguished. They adopted the verse divisions of the Geneva Bible, but avoided marginal notes. The Bishops' Bible was published in 1568 in one folio volume.

The main frontispiece depicts Queen Elizabeth in her robes of state and accompanied by the royal arms. Many woodcuts, maps, and copperplate engravings illustrate the book. Preceding the book of Joshua, a subordinate title page contains an engraved portrait of Elizabeth's favorite, the Earl of Leicester, and an engraved portrait of Cecil, Lord Burleigh, appears in front of the Psalms. Some of the ornamental initials, throughout the work, contain portraits of William Cecil, Secretary of State, and Archbishop Parker; other initials contain various coats of arms.

The bishops failed, however, in their apparent attempt to couple obedience to God with absolute loyalty to the English monarch. Although an English Church Convocation, in 1571, ordered all church wardens to obtain a copy for their churches, the Bishops' Bible, born out of prejudice against the popularity of the Geneva Bible, never gained wide acceptance among the people.

The New Testament was printed on thicker paper to withstand greater use; but it was expensive, selling for 27 shillings and eight pence—far more than most could afford. Especially unpopular were the symbols of pagan mythology included on the frontispiece of the second edition. The last printing of the Bishops' Bible appeared in 1606, five years before the King James Version made its debut. A curious marginal note at Psalm 45:9 reads, "Ophir is thought to be the Ilande in the west coast, of late founde by Christopher Columbo, from whence at this day is brought most fine gold."

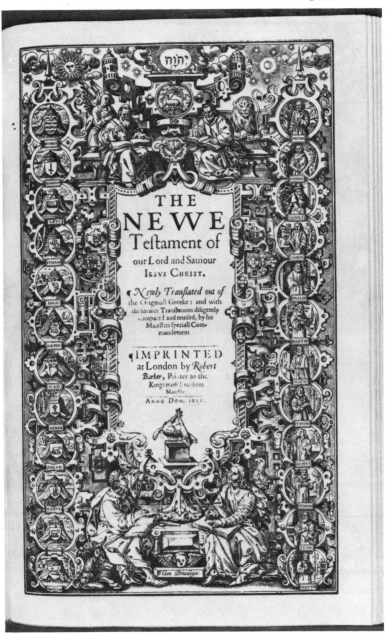

King James (Authorized) Version of 1611. New Testament title page.

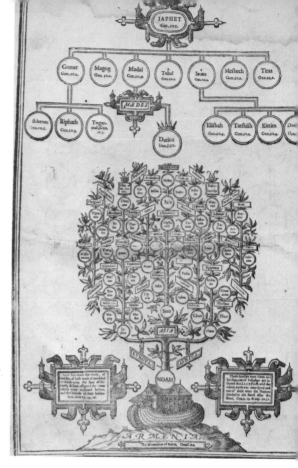

King James (Authorized) Version of 1611. Chart showing the divisions of people in the earth after the flood. This diagram appears also in the KJV of 1613.

The King James Bible

"**I** could never yet see a Bible well translated in English; but I think that, of all, that of Geneva is the worst," spoke King James I of England in 1604. Queen Elizabeth had died in 1603, and the kingdom which she left—so poor and defenseless at the beginning of her reign—had in 45 years become a rich and mighty realm, the beginning of a vast empire. But Elizabeth left no heir, and the throne of England passed from the Tudors to the Stuarts. By 1604 there was a growing concern among Protestants for the numerous mistranslations in the *Book of Common Prayer*, and many felt that the time was ripe for a new translation.

Actually, the Geneva Bible (1560), most popular among Puritans and Scottish Presbyterians, had corrected many of the earlier mistranslations; however, James I rejected it because of the conspicuous republicanism in the marginal notes, which he described as "partial, untrue, and seditious, savouring too much of dangerous and traitorous conceits." He referred to such notes as the one at Exodus 1:19, which depicts the midwives' disobedience to Pharaoh as "lawful." Especially contrary to James' doctrine of the "divine right of kings" was the marginal note at II Chronicles 15:16, where Asa deposes his wicked mother, Queen Maachah, for her idolatry. The Geneva note says, "Herein [Asa] showed that he lacked zeal: for she ought to have died . . . but he gave place to foolish pity." This sharply offended James, whose own mother was Mary, the wicked Queen of Scots whom the fiery John Knox had more than once exhorted and rebuked. James, who for 37 years had been James VI of Scotland, had come to despise any form of Presbyterianism. This was the situation when, at the famous Hampton Court Conference on January 14, 1604, the distinguished Puritan Dr. John Rainolds (Reynolds)—learned president of Corpus Christi College at Oxford—"moved his Majestie, that there might bee a newe translation of the Bible."

The names of proposed translators were submitted to King James, who in July 1604 announced that he had appointed 54 learned men to translate the Bible into English. When the work formally began in 1607, the number of translators actually engaged in the work was about 47, and of these several died before the work's completion. These men were the best biblical scholars and linguists of their day—men of profound and unaffected piety. The revisers were divided into three groups (each consisting of two companies) at Westminster, Oxford, and Cambridge. In the Jerusalem Chamber at Westminster, one company (of ten) translated Genesis through II Kings, and another company (of seven) translated Romans through Jude. At Cambridge, one company (of eight) completed I Chronicles through Ecclesiastes, while a second company (of seven) translated the entire Apocrypha. At Oxford, one company (of seven) was responsible for Isaiah through Malachi, while a second company (of eight) rendered the Gospels, Acts, and the Apocalypse.

Each translator worked, first of all, individually on an assigned chapter or small portion of Scripture; he then submitted his work to his colleagues for review and necessary revision. Leaving nothing to individual fancy, but drawing from the collective wisdom of a host of counselors, each company, as soon as it had collectively completed its rendering of any one book, sent a transcript of it to each of the other five companies. Carelessness found no place in this project. Each company was under the direction of an eminent churchman: the Regius Professors of Hebrew and Greek at Oxford University directed the two companies there; their counterparts at Cambridge directed the work there; and the Dean of Westminster, along with the Dean of Chester, supervised the two Westminster companies. Eventually, 12 delegates—two from each of the six companies—met together daily for nine months at Stationers' Hall, London, as a revision committee, each member of which received from the King's Printer, Robert Barker, a remuneration of 30 shillings a week. For the original translators, however, nothing more than room and board at the universities was stipulated. A final revision committee consisted of two: Dr. Miles Smith (one of the translators and the probable author of the Translators' Preface) and Thomas Bilson, Bishop of Winchester, who was not one of the regular translators.

Provided for the revisers' guidance was a set of 15 rules (probably drafted by Richard Bancroft, Archbishop of Canterbury), the first of which stipulated that the Bishops' Bible was to be followed, "and as little altered as the truth of the original will admit." The fourteenth rule instructed that the following Bibles could be followed when they agreed better with the text than the Bishops' Bible: Tyndale's, Matthew's, Coverdale's, the Great Bible, and the Geneva Bible. The finished product, however, was more than a simple revision of the Bishops' Bible; it was, as its title page indicates, a "newly translated" Bible. The Translators' Preface modestly explains: "Truly . . . we never thought . . . to make a new Translation, nor yet to make of a bad one a good one; but to make a good one better, or out of many good ones one principal good one." The translators committed themselves to specially-designed regulations which ensured that the new revision would not become a sectarian Bible. "Old ecclesiastical words" were to remain; for example, the word *church* could not be translated *congregation*. The Greek word for *baptism* was transliterated, not translated. When a word had "divers signification," that was to be kept "which hath been most commonly used by the most of the ancient fathers." They could include no marginal notes, except for brief explanations of difficult Hebrew and Greek words which could not be translated meaningfully. In the Preface, these eminent translators praise the previous English versions. Even the "meanest" translation "containeth the word of God, nay, is the word of God: as the King's speech which he uttered in Parliament, being translated into French, Dutch, Italian, and Latin is still the King's speech, though it be not interpreted by every translator with like grace. . . . But we weary the unlearned, who need not know so much; and trouble the learned, who know it already."

In 1611 Robert Barker, "Printer to the King's Most Excellent Majesty," presented to the public the handsome production 1500 pages in length and over three inches thick (including the binding). This masterpiece measures 16½ x 10½—almost as large as the Great Bible. The type is set in double columns. The title page reads,

The Holy Bible, Conteyning the Old Testament, and the New: Newly Translated out of the Originall tongues: & with the former Translations diligently compared and revised, by his Majesties Special Commandment. Appointed to be read in Churches. Imprinted at London by Robert Barker, Printer to the Kings most Excellent Majestie, Anno Dom. 1611.

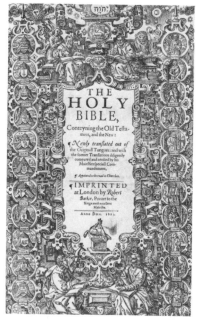

King James (Authorized) edition of 1613. Front title page.

This title forms the center of an engraving showing the figures of Moses and Aaron to the right and to the left respectively. At the top of this title page, in Hebrew characters, is God's covenant name—Jehovah. Under this is the sacred dove, which is symbolic of the Holy Spirit— the Author of Holy Writ. Under the dove is the lamb, symbolic of Christ, who once instructed, "Search the scriptures; for ... they are they which testify of me" (John 5:39). At each of the four corners is one of the four Gospel writers: the symbol of a man portrays Matthew, a lion signifies Mark, an ox symbolizes Luke, and an eagle denotes John. The symbols are based upon Revelation 4:6-10. At the bottom of the page, a pelican is "vulning" herself, that is, wounding herself with her beak to feed her young with her own blood, thus symbolizing the redeeming work of Christ. Below the pelican is the artist's signature: *"C. Boel fecit in Richmont."* The New Testament bears a separate title:

> The Newe Testament of our Lord and Saviour Jesus Christ. Newly translated out of the Originall Greeke; and with the former Translations diligently compared and revised, by his Majesties speciall Commandment. Imprinted at London by Robert Barker, Printer to the Kings most Excellent Majestie. Anno Dom. 1611.

In vertical columns, this title page depicts the 12 tribes of Israel on the left and the 12 apostles on the right. This King James Bible of 1611 includes genealogies, maps, headline summaries, chapter summaries, numbered verses, paragraph signs (up to Acts 20:36, where they curiously disappear), cross references, and brief philological marginal notes. The words, "Appointed to be read in Churches," probably meant to Barker that, as the copies of the Bishops' Bible wore out, churches would replace them with this new translation; therefore, the editors inserted a profusion of commas to aid in public reading. Incidentally, the King James Version was the last Protestant translation to include the Apocrypha until recent times.

The first edition required 20,000 copies, but no printing office in England in 1611 could fill such an order; consequently, Barker made two impressions (or issues) of this edition to hasten its production. Even these two initial editions contain significant variations, the most famous of which occurs at Ruth 3:15. In the first folio, the verse reads, ". . . and he [Boaz] measured six measures of barley, and laide it on her: and he went into the Citie." The other folio renders the last phrase, ". . . and *she* [Ruth] went into the citie." The issues soon came to be known as "the Great He Bible" and "the Great She Bible" respectively. The original folios sold for about 25 shillings each. Which of the two original editions ("He" or "She") is the more completely "correct" is debatable, for the printers of that day often bound together sheets from different printings as copy for new editions, thus accelerating the spawning of error. According to the catalogue of the British and Foreign Bible Society, the number of editions of the King James Bible (or parts of it) between 1611 and 1800 reached nearly a thousand and produced tens of thousands of minor variations from the original edition.

This was the superlative English translation of the Word of Life. As a matter of fact, the very authorization of this "Authorized Version" came from the popular acclamation of the English-speaking world gradually "authorizing" it on the basis of its own merits and integrity. Although some vigorously opposed it for years, the venerable King James Version eventually replaced even the popular Geneva Bible. The King James translation of the Gospels and Epistles replaced the Geneva translation in the *Book of Common Prayer* in 1661.

The 1611 editions contain some peculiarities: the incomplete translation, "Thou art Christ" (Matthew 16:16), did not become "Thou art *the* Christ" until 1762, when correctors also changed the statement in Matthew 26:75, "And Peter remembered the *words* of Jesus," to "the *word* of Jesus"; the phrase in Mark 2:4, "And when they could not come nigh unto him for preasse" became in 1743, "for *the* press"; Luke 1:3, "it seemed good to me also, having had perfect understanding of things from the very first" became in 1629, "understanding of *all* things"; and John 15:20, "the servant is not greater than *the* Lord" became in 1762, "the servant is not greater than *his* lord." Many mistranslations remain in the King James: for example *"after* three *years"* (Amos 4:4) should be *"every* three *days"*; "strain *at* a gnat" (Matthew 23:24) should be "strain *out* a gnat"; "between the *temple* and the altar" (Matthew 23:35) should read, "between the *sanctuary* and the altar"; "thieves" (Mark 15:27) should be "bandits"; and "Art thou *a master* of Israel" (John 3:10) should be "Art thou *the teacher* of Israel?" These are only a few of the literally dozens of minor mistranslations which remain to this day. Obviously, the King James translators' scholarship, like all others, was not impeccable. Their knowledge of the ancient languages was defective in regard to tenses and idioms and they had no papyri to aid them with *Koine* Greek—the dialect of the Greek New Testament.

In spite of its imperfect translation, the English style of the King James Version has always merited great praise. Remarkable for the majesty and rhythm of Elizabethan English, "the music of the English Bible" has become proverbial. The translators exhibit on every page their perfect and easy command over the English language. "As a whole their work was done most carefully and honestly," remarks B. F. Westcott, "even in the minutest details the translation is that of a Church and not of a party. . . . No kind of emendation appears to have been neglected, and almost every change was an improvement." It is true that the three most ancient and significant Greek manuscripts were not available to the King James revisers: *Codex Vaticanus* was still hidden by the Vatican authorities, *Codex Sinaiticus* was discovered more than two and a half centuries later, and *Codex Alexandrinus* became known in the West shortly after the publication of the King James Bible. Nevertheless, the translators utilized every accessible tool. They had two valuable aids which were not available to their predecessors: the Antwerp Polyglot of 1572 and Tremellius's Bible of 1579. In addition, the King James translators had before them a great many other versions, including Luther's German translation. They even had Italian and Spanish translations and several Latin versions. They used the best Hebrew and Greek manuscripts available at that time. Even the Syriac New Testament and the Aramaic Targums were available. In both equipment and method of translation, the King James was produced according to the highest standards of scholarship and the most advanced knowledge available in that day. The translators themselves, in their Preface, humbly describe the benefits of such work:

> Translation it is that openeth the window, to let in the light; that breaketh the shell, that we may eat the kernell; that putteth aside the curtain, that we may look into the most holy place; that removeth the cover of the well, that we may come by the water.

In 1612, Robert Barker made handy quarto and octavo editions of the King James Bible available for quick sale. Although seldom recognized for their contribution, Christopher and Robert Barker, through mass producing inexpensive Bibles, enabled thousands of English homes which were otherwise practically bookless to have a book of high spiritual and literary quality. Ultimately, they provided the American colonies with literate settlers, better fitted for self-government. It is ironic that King James, in his endeavor to replace the Geneva Bible (with its hard-hitting notes), substituted for it an unannotated

Bible which inevitably encouraged its readers to independence of thought. So a king (whom the French called "the wisest fool in Christendom"), in order to protect his doctrine of "the divine right of kings," caused the publication of a best-seller—"the noblest book in the English language"—which became a milestone in the march of American republicanism.

The King James Bible (1613 Edition)

Between 1611 and 1614 the King James Bible went into 17 editions. In the 1613 edition there are more than 300 variations from the two original 1611 editions. For example, the "He" edition of 1611 had reduplicated three lines of Exodus 14:10, but the 1613 edition corrected this. In the same folio of 1611, the chapter heading for II Samuel 24 reads "eleven thousand;" the 1613 edition corrects this to read "thirteen hundred thousand." The second folio (the "She") of 1611 has "Judas" in place of "Jesus" in Matthew 26:36—"Then cometh Jesus with them unto a place called Gethsemane." Other corrections in the 1613 edition include the following: "hoopes" (in Exodus 38:10) now becomes "hookes"; "the plaine be" (in Leviticus 13:56) is now "the plague be"; "ye shall not eat" (Leviticus 17:14) reads, "ye shall eat"; and "lost his his life" (Matthew 16:25) now reads, "lose his life." Some peculiarities of the 1611 editions remained unchanged in 1613; for example, the words *of God* remain omitted from the familiar phrase in I John 5:12, "he that hath not the Son of God." Also, the word *Amorite* remains misspelled—"Emorite"—in Genesis 10:16. Robert Barker, the printer of the 1611 editions, also printed this 1613 edition, which having smaller type and fewer folio leaves, was intended for the "poorer churches."

The King James Bible (1638 Edition)

The most important of the 182 editions of the King James Bible published between 1611 and 1644 was the 1638 edition. This is the first Cambridge edition in folio and is generally very well done. For the first time, the words *of*

God are correctly included in I John 5:12: "he that hath not the Son of God." The older King James Versions had rendered Mark 5:6, "But when hee saw Jesus afarre off, he *came* and worshipped him." Now, in 1638, the passage more precisely reads, "he *ranne* and worshipped." The printers, Thomas Burk and Robert Daniel, carefully avoided the kinds of error made by the printers of a 1631 edition, dubbed the "Wicked Bible" for its rendering of the seventh commandment as "Thou shalt commit adultery." A similar type of error led to the naming of a 1653 edition, the "Unrighteous Bible," which says in I Corinthians 6:9, "the unrighteous shall inherit the kingdom of God." Cotton Mather, complaining in 1702 of "Scandalous Errors of the Press-work," through which "The Holy Bible itself . . . hath been affronted," mentions one edition which expresses the problem very artistically: it makes Psalm 119:161 read, "Printers [Princes] have persecuted me without a cause."

In the King James edition of 1638, however, only a few new errors appear, the most significant occurring at Acts 6:3, which it renders, "Wherefore brethren, look ye out among you seven men of honest report, full of the holy Ghost and wisdome, whom *ye* may appoint. . . ." The last phrase should have read, "whom *we* may appoint." This alteration has often been ascribed to Oliver Cromwell, who allegedly bribed the printers with 1000 pounds to make the change, which would give the appearance of biblical support for the appointment of ministers *by the people.* Both Anglicans and Scottish Presbyterians abhorred such polity. The appearance of this error in a 1638 edition refutes the allegation, however, because Charles I himself ordered this complete revision four years prior to England's Civil War. On the whole, this new edition shows evidence of extensive and careful revision, and it remained the standard text of the King James Version for well over a century.

Surely, the extent of influence—both immediate and permanent—which the King James Version has had on English literature cannot be exaggerated. Moreover, the

English language will continue to change; language grows and fades like a flower. How encouraging to know that, although "the flower falleth away," the "Word of the Lord endureth forever."

Three Famous Greek Manuscripts

Since the publication of the King James Version in 1611, numerous manuscript discoveries have contributed to a vastly increased knowledge of the original Scripture languages—Hebrew and Greek. Although many findings, such as the famous *Codex Ephraemi,* or even the Dead Sea Scrolls, deserve attention, the three most significant extant contributions toward the advancement of textual learning are *Codex Alexandrinus, Codex Vaticanus,* and *Codex Sinaiticus.* The word *codex* is the Latin word for *book* and is often used synonymously with the word *manuscript.* Highly esteemed by all biblical scholars for their worth and antiquity, these manuscripts remain among the chief treasures of the ancient world. They were written in Greek capital letters called "uncials" on vellum (animal skins); these letters have no spacing and little or no punctuation— PRINTEDINENGLISHTHEYWOULDLOOKLIKETHIS.

Codex Alexandrinus (Codex A) A.D. 400-450
In 1625, Cyril Lucar, the reforming patriarch of Constantinople, offered to King James I of England an ancient Greek manuscript of the Scriptures; this was only 14 years after the publication of the King James Bible. Lucar who had been patriarch of Alexandria, Egypt, had brought the manuscript known as *Codex Alexandrinus* with him to Constantinople. King James died before it could be delivered, so Cyril Lucar presented it to King Charles I through Sir Thomas Roe, British Ambassador at Constantinople.

Many believe that *Codex Alexandrinus* is the work of a company of five scribes. It consists of four volumes—the first three containing the Old Testament and the fourth containing the New Testament, with the epistles of Clement of Rome, an epistle of Athanasius, and a work of Eusebius on the Psalms. Although a few pages are now missing, the original comprised 773 parchment leaves—each measuring approximately 12⅝" x 10⅜". Each leaf has two columns, and each column runs irregularly from 46 to 52 lines—the average page length being 50 or 51 lines. The scribes conveniently enlarged the initial letter of each paragraph and, except in the poetical books, placed it in the margin. They used red ink for the titles of the Psalms and for the first line or two of each book. The manuscript's only missing sections are Matthew 1:1 to 25:6, John 6:50 to 8:52, and II Corinthians 4:13 to 12:6. Brian Walton (c. 1600-1661) used *Codex Alexandrinus* in his famous six-volume *Biblia Sacra Polyglotta*. Since 1757, *Codex Alexandrinus* has been

Codex Alexandrinus (Codex A). Ancient manuscript which dates to about A.D. 400-450. This leaf contains I John 4:4—5:9. The controversial passage—5:7b and 8a of the Authorized Version—does not appear in such early manuscripts.

in the royal library of the British Museum, which published, from 1879 to 1883, a photographic reproduction of the manuscript. In 1909 F. G. Kenyon began publishing a reduced five-part facsimile of the noted manuscript.

Codex Vaticanus (Codex B) A.D. 350

This manuscript, which brings modern scholarship in touch with the days of Constantine, first became available through the fortunes of war. Napoleon seized the document from the Vatican as a war prize and transported it to Paris, where it rapidly gained the attention of biblical scholars. *Codex Vaticanus* was returned to Rome in 1815 where it remains the property of the Vatican Library. A catalogue of this library listed the manuscript as early as 1475, but for centuries the popes guarded it closely and prevented its recognition. Romanism has specialized in suppressing truth. The popes obviously believed that *Codex Vaticanus* posed a potential threat to their "inspired" Latin Vulgate, the Roman Catholic church's official version. The great English scholar, Samuel Prideaux Tregelles (1813-1875), visited the Vatican about 1843 to study *Codex Vaticanus*. After enduring five months of empty promises and weary delays, he left Rome without accomplishing his task.

"It is true," explained Tregelles later, in a lecture delivered before the Plymouth Young Men's Christian Association, "that I often saw the MS., but they would not allow me to use it; and they would not let me open it without searching my pockets, and depriving me of pen, ink, and paper; and at the same time two *prelati* kept me in constant conversation in Latin, and if I looked at a passage too long, they would snatch the book out of my hand. So foolishly and meaninglessly did the papal authorities seek to keep this precious MS. to themselves."

After *Vaticanus's* initial exposure to scholarly examination, however, constant requests for its availability bombarded the Vatican authorities. Finally, Cardinal Angelo Mai published editions of it in 1857 and 1859. Ten

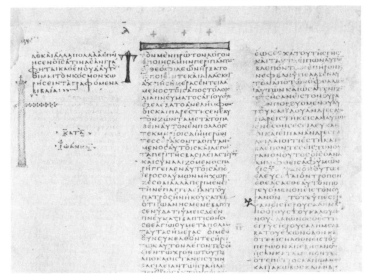

Codex Vaticanus (Codex B). Ancient copyists, about A.D. 350, produced this priceless manuscript on the finest vellum—said to be antelope skin. On this leaf, the first column contains John 21:25; the second column contains Acts 1:1-8a; and the third contains Acts 1:8b-15.

years later, Constantin von Tischendorf published his revised and corrected *Novum Testamentum Vaticanum*. Vercellone and Cozza published still another edition in 1868-1869. In 1889-1890, a complete photographic facsimile of the whole manuscript, edited by Giuseppe Cozza-Luzi, appeared. A facsimile edition of the New Testament portion was issued at Milan, between 1904 and 1907. In 1965 Pope Paul VI ordered still another photographic reproduction of the New Testament section of *Codex Vaticanus* and presented copies of it to the members and observers of Vatican Council II. Since such a gesture was intended to improve the pope's and the Roman church's public image, copies soon became widely available.

In spite of its title, *Codex Vaticanus* is not a "Roman Catholic manuscript"; ancient scribes carefully produced this treasure long before there was a "Roman Catholic" church and certainly before there was any "pope." No one knows how or when the document arrived at the Vatican where the apostate Church of Rome suppressed it for so long; nevertheless, God has graciously opened a door that no man can shut: God has made it possible for thousands of copies of this gem to be disseminated among Bible-believing scholars. Written on the finest vellum—said to be antelope skin—the manuscript originally consisted of about 820 leaves, of which 759 survive. Each leaf measures 10½" x 10" and contains three columns of 42 lines. The Old Testament is complete except for the first part of Genesis and some of the psalms. The New Testament books are in this order: the four Gospels, Acts, James, I and II Peter, I, II, and III John, Jude, Romans, I and II Corinthians, Galatians, Ephesians, Philippians, Colossians, I and II Thessalonians, and Hebrews as far as 9:14. (I and II Timothy, Titus, Philemon, Hebrews 9:15-13:25, and Revelation are missing).

Codex Sinaiticus (Codex Aleph) A.D. 300-350

Constantin von Tischendorf (1815-1875)—German Protestant, Leipzig University professor, earnest textual scholar, polished theologian, and Christian philologist—devoted his life to the discovery of the oldest surviving biblical manuscripts. His love for the sacred text was the motivating force of his life; he published more editions of the New Testament text than any other scholar. Most valuable of all of these editions is his famous *Novum Testamentum Graece* (Greek New Testament, 1869-1872). This two-volume *editio octava critica maior* remains an enormous tool for the serious student of the New Testament; the work stands as the compilation of a lifetime of sacrificial work by a master-mind and spiritual giant. Tischendorf's numerous earlier editions included the noted *Codex Ephraemi Rescriptus* (1843-1845), *Codex Amiatinus* (1850), and *Codex Claromontanus* (1852); his most famous discovery, however, was the *Codex Sinaiticus*.

The story of *Codex Sinaiticus*'s discovery began when Tischendorf visited numerous eastern monasteries searching in dusty libraries for ancient manuscripts that had survived the passing centuries. One day in May

Novum Testamentum Graece.
Published 1869-1872, this Greek
New Testament is the most valuable
of Constantin von Tischendorf's
numerous editions. This section,
from volume one, contains
John 10:18b-22a.

1844, he was about to leave St. Catherine's Monastery at the base of Mt. Sinai when he noticed, in the middle of the great hall, a basket of old parchments. The librarian explained that the monks used these sheets to light the oven fires and that they had already burned two basketfuls of similar "rubbish." Examining the basket's contents, Tischendorf discovered 129 leaves of a Septuagint Bible—the Greek Old Testament. Tischendorf became excited, and the monks became suspicious; they did, however, permit the scholar to keep one-third (43) of these parchments, which contained portions of I Chronicles, Jeremiah, Nehemiah, and Esther. Returning to Europe, Tischendorf deposited the manuscripts in the Leipzig University Library, and two years later he published their contents, which he named *Codex Frederico-Augustanus* (in honor of his patron, Frederick Augustus, the King of Saxony). Tischendorf returned to Mt. Sinai in 1853, but the visit was fruitless; his previous display of emotion had made the monks more cautious than to expose their treasures to a European traveler.

In 1856, Tischendorf submitted to the Czar of Russia, Alexander II, a plan for making systematic researches in the East. Approval and necessary funds came two years later; finally, in January 1859, under the official patronage of Alexander II, Tischendorf returned to Mt. Sinai for his third visit. Wiser from experience, Tischendorf diplomatically waited until the closing days of his visit to casually show the steward of the monastery a copy of the earlier-discovered manuscripts which he had published at Leipzig. Thereupon, the steward remarked that he too had a copy of the Scriptures and produced from a closet in his cell a manuscript, wrapped in red cloth. Tischendorf, concealing his excitement, casually asked permission to take it to his room that evening. "I knew that I held in my hand the most precious Biblical treasure in existence," Tischendorf later testified, "a document whose age and importance exceeded that of all the manuscripts which I had ever examined during twenty years' study of the subject." This was the most exciting moment in Tischendorf's entire life; he stayed up all night, fathoming his newly-found treasure. In his diary, the scholar writes, *"Quippe dormire nefas videbatur"* ("It really seemed a sacrilege to sleep").

Tischendorf noticed that his soon-to-be-called *Codex Sinaiticus* contained a large portion of the Old Testament, the complete New Testament, the *Epistle of Barnabas*, and part of the *Shepherd of Hermas*. Each of these vellum parchments measures about 14⅞" x 13½" and has four columns of writing—each column consists of exactly 48 lines. "Is it possible," pondered Tischendorf, "that this Bible could be one of the 50 copies which Emperor Constantine ordered Eusebius to place in Constantinople, his new capital?" After trying unsuccessfully to buy the manuscript, Tischendorf went to Cairo, where the monks of Sinai had another small monastery, and petitioned the abbot for the priceless document. Sending swift Bedouin messengers to bring the manuscript to Cairo, the abbot allowed Tischendorf access to it, "quire by quire" (eight leaves at a time), that he might copy it. Aided by two Germans (an apothecary and a bookseller), Tischendorf carefully transcribed the entire manuscript—all 110,000 lines—in two months.

At this time there was a vacancy in St. Catherine's highest authoritative office—the archbishopric. Tischen-

*Codex Sinaiticus (Aleph). Ancient manuscript which dates to about A.D. 300-350.
This leaf contains Romans 8:38b-10:1a.*

dorf tactfully suggested to the Sinai monks that it would be
to their advantage to make a gift of the manuscript to the
Czar of Russia—the natural protector of the Greek
Orthodox churches. The idea of having the Czar's
influence was appealing. After a series of negotiations, the
monks presented the assembled manuscript to the Czar,
who placed it in the Imperial Library at St. Petersburg. In
1862 (the one thousandth anniversary of the founding of
the Russian Empire), the Russian government financed the
publishing (at Leipzig, Germany) of a magnificent 300-
copy edition of *Codex Sinaiticus* in four folio volumes, with 21
plates of actual facsimiles. In 1869 the Czar finally
remunerated the monks: to the Mt. Sinai monks, he
presented 7000 rubles for their library and a silver shrine
for St. Catherine; to the Cairo monks, the Czar gave 2000
rubles and several Russian decorations (similar to
honorary degrees). The 9000 rubles in that day were equal
to about $7000.

Finally, Oxford University Press issued beautiful, well-bound facsimiles of *Codex Sinaiticus* from photographs taken at St. Petersburg by Professor Kirsopp Lake. The New Testament appeared in 1911 and the Old Testament in 1922. After the Bolshevik Revolution of 1917, the original manuscript passed into the hands of the Soviet government, which, having no interest in the Bible, sold it to the British Museum in 1933 for 100,000 pounds, which at that time was equivalent to about a half million dollars. Today, *Codex Sinaiticus* remains, along with *Codex Alexandrinus*, in the British Museum's Department of Manuscripts. In 1981 the monks at St. Catherine's tore down a wall of their ancient monastery and discovered thousands of priceless fragments and parchments, including eight of *Codex Sinaiticus*'s previously-missing leaves.

Brian Walton's Biblia Sacra Polyglotta

Brian Walton (1600-1661) was born in Yorkshire and educated at Cambridge. He became involved in the intricate troubles between the regular clergy and the Puritans, arguing, for example, that the parishioners were not paying their legally-required tithes, which supported the clergy. Walton generally won the favor of the established clergy, but became obnoxious to the Puritans, who asserted that unworthy ministers did not deserve the tithe. Walton further alienated the Puritans by agreeing with Archbishop Laud, who favored removing the communion tables from the center of the churches to the east side, where protective rails could guard the tables from dogs and other animals, which often wandered unnoticed into the open churches. To the parishioners who had previously enjoyed fellowship "around the Lord's table," such a change barred them from any direct approach. The Puritans thought there were more appropriate means of protecting the tables from the alleged threat of dogs.

The six-volume *Biblia Sacra Polyglotta* was Brian Walton's best-known work. The printing began in 1653, and between 1654 and 1657 all six volumes appeared. Volumes I-IV contain the Old Testament and the Apocrypha; Volume V has the New Testament, and Volume VI consists of various critical appendices. Although no single book of Scripture in Walton's Polyglot appears in more than eight languages, this "London Polyglot"—as it came to be known—includes nine languages. The type characters, all of English make, rendered the finished product the typographical achievement of the century. Walton's was the fourth, the most accurate, and the most comprehensive of the great Polyglots. With this work, the student can see the Old Testament text in such languages as Hebrew, Latin, Chaldee, Syriac, and Aramaic—all in well-arranged columns. The New Testament appears in Greek, Latin, Syriac, Ethiopic, Arabic, and (for the Gospels) Persian. The Greek text, with slight alterations, is that of Robert Stephanus (Estienne); this so-called Stevens' Text, because of its reliance upon Erasmus' text, is also called the English *Textus Receptus* (Received Text). Underneath the Greek sections, however, Walton provides the variant readings from *Codex Alexandrinus*. In the appendix he provides the variant readings of 16 authorities, including *Codex Alexandrinus*. As an added help to the student of his Polyglot, Walton in 1655 published his *Introductio ad Lectionem Linguarum Orientalium*.

Because the "high churchman" first published his set during Oliver Cromwell's Protectorate, no "dedicatory" page appears. The Puritans remained suspicious of Walton; in fact Dr. John Owen wrote a lengthy and controversial critique of Walton's prolegomena and appendices to the Polyglot Bible. After the Stuart Restoration, Walton dedicated the Polyglot to King Charles II, who appointed him Chaplain to the King in 1660—the same year in which

Walton became Bishop of Chester. Walton's Polyglot is one of the earliest books published by private subscription (in this case—ten pounds a set). In 1669 Dr. Edmund Castell prepared a two-volume *Heptaglot Lexicon* to serve as a valuable supplement to the Polyglot; it explains the oriental languages in Walton's work.

Brian Walton's Biblia Sacra Polyglotta. With this handy device, published in 1654-1657, the scholar who knew Latin could now also discuss the Oriental languages such as Hebrew and Aramaic. Walton provides an interlinear Hebrew text with the Latin translation. This passage shows a section from Exodus 20.

The Massorah

The term *Massorah* means "tradition" (that which has been handed down). The word refers to the notes that Jewish scholars, called Masoretes, made in order to preserve the correct spelling and pronunciation of the words in the Old Testament Hebrew text. They were particularly active from the sixth to the tenth centuries, A.D. Although its roots go back to the time of Ezra, we trace our present Masoretic system itself almost entirely to Aaron ben Asher (ninth century), the most prominent of the Masoretic scholars. Since biblical Hebrew was written without vowels and had ceased to be a spoken tongue, the introduction of a vowel system in the eighth century became especially significant to future Hebrew scholars. The Masoretes took this vowel system and very reverently sought to give each Old Testament Hebrew word its exact grammatical form and pronunciation. The many possible renderings of Hebrew consonants without vowels illustrate the immense value of the Masoretes' achievement. For example, the consonants MLK could be read, according to context, *melek* (king), *malak* (he reigned), *molek* (reigning), *malok* (to reign), or even *Molek* (the idol). Again, the consonants DBR could read, according to the context, *dober* (speaking), *dabar* (he spoke, or a word), or *deber* (a pestilence, or a thorn).

In the margins of the text, the Masoretes placed variant

Hebrew manuscript. Ninth-century A.D. manuscript with the Massorah in its upper and lower, as well as its side and middle, columns. This three-columned page contains Numbers 26:12-27.

readings, called *qere* (what is to be read). The reading of the text itself is called the *kethib* (what is written). The best-known example of a Masoretic *qere* is God's covenant name, Jehovah, whose four Hebrew consonants, called the *tetragrammaton*, are YHWH. The Jews always substituted for this ineffable name the title "Lord" (*Adonai*) because they feared to mispronounce God's personal and covenant name. The Masoretes indicated this substitution by inserting the vowels of *Adonai* under the consonants YHWH; this combination resulted in the word *Yehowah* (or *Jehovah*, as the Authorized Version renders it). Correctly pronounced the original word comes out as *Yahweh*. God's name was so holy and sacred that the ancient scribes would not write it with a freshly dipped pen, lest the ink spatter.

The Masoretes' great contribution was their standardization of the Hebrew text. The text that we use today is the Masoretic text, in contrast to the text underlying such early translations as the Septuagint. So closely did the Masoretes seek to guard the text against all error that even when they felt that a word should be changed, they left the original consonants undisturbed; they simply inserted the vowel points of the new word and placed the consonants of the new word in the margin. The Masoretes bring us very close, in all essentials, to the original autographs themselves. These scholars even counted all the verses, words, and letters of each book of the Old Testament and appended these figures at the end of each book to advance the minute study, not only of every word of God, but of every jot and tittle. A jot (*yod*) is the smallest Hebrew letter, and a tittle is the smallest part of a letter that can change its identification. "For verily I say unto you, Till heaven and earth pass, one jot or one tittle shall in no wise pass from the law, till all be fulfilled" (Matthew 5:18). For many of our convenient tools of Bible study, we can thank the Masoretes, who encouraged careful analytical study of God's Word.

English Translation from the Peshitta Text

The Peshitta text is in the Aramaic-Syriac language which the ancients in Syria and Mesopotamia used; it is sometimes called Eastern Aramaic to distinguish it from the closely-related Western Aramaic, which was spoken in Palestine during our Lord's earthly ministry. The word *Peshitta* means "simple." The Peshitta New Testament was in use in the fifth century; in fact, there is a Peshitta Bible of A.D. 464 in the British Museum. The Peshitta text is the authorized Bible of the Eastern churches and is often called the "Syriac Vulgate." Approximately 350 manuscripts of the text survive; the earliest of these dates from the fifth and sixth centuries. The Peshitta text omits the account of the woman taken in adultery in John 8; it also omits the books of II Peter, II and III John, Jude, and Revelation.

In 1940 George M. Lamsa's English translation from the Peshitta text appeared under the title *The New Testament According to the Eastern Text;* Lamsa describes his translation as taken "from original Aramaic sources." Lamsa's entire Bible translation appeared in 1957; he claims that it represents the "original Eastern text of both the New and Old Testaments." Although his work is interesting and in some ways commendable, Lamsa's presuppositions are contrary to most scholarly opinion. The facts are well-established that, contrary to Lamsa's assertions, Hebrew is the original language of most of the Old Testament and that Greek is the original language of most of the New. Claiming that Aramaic was the original language of both Testaments, George Lamsa boldly asserts that "Jesus and his disciples not only could not converse in Greek, but they never heard it spoken" (p. ix). In his translation, Lamsa includes the New Testament portions omitted in the Peshitta text; for these portions, he uses Aramaic texts from a much later period. Lamsa was born in Kurdistan,

I will break the Assyrian ...   711   ISAIAH 15

8 Yea, the fir trees rejoice over you, and the cedars of Lebanon, saying, Since you are felled, no hewer is come up to cut us down.

9 Sheol beneath is murmuring at your coming; it stirs up against you all the mighty men, even all the rulers of the earth whom you overthrew from their thrones.

10 All the kings of the nations shall answer and say to you, Are you also become weak as we? Are you become like us?

11 Your pomp is brought down to Sheol, the noise of your harps is dead; the dust is spread under you, and the worms cover you.

12 How are you fallen from heaven! howl in the morning! for you have fallen down to the ground, O reviler of the nations.

13 For you have said in your heart, I will ascend into heaven, I will exalt my throne above the stars of God; I will dwell also upon the high mountains in the outer regions of the

dren for the iniquity of their fathers; that they do not rise, nor possess the land, nor fill the face of the world with war.

22 For I will rise up against them, says the LORD of hosts, and will cut off from Babylon the name, its offspring, the family, and its generation, says the LORD.

23 I will also make it a possession for owls, and pools of water; and I will sweep it with the broom of destruction, says the LORD of hosts.

24 ¶The LORD of hosts has sworn, saying, Surely as I have thought, so shall it come to pass; and as I have purposed, so shall it stand;

25 I will break the Assyrian in my land, and upon my mountains tread him under foot; then his yoke shall depart from off them, and his burden depart from off their shoulders.

26 This is the end that is purposed against all the earth; and this is the land that is stretched out against all the nations.

English translation from the Peshitta text. George M. Lamsa, who rendered this unusual translation from the Aramaic, falsely asserts that "Jesus and his disciples not only could not converse in Greek but they never heard it spoken." Shown here is his rendering of Isaiah 14:12.

where an Aramaic dialect prevails. A close examination of his English translation reveals Lamsa's great indebtedness to the King James Version; he also relied heavily upon the American Standard Version of 1901. An interesting departure from the English translations, however, occurs in Isaiah 14:12. The King James translation reads, "How art thou fallen from heaven, O Lucifer, son of the morning!" Lamsa leaves Lucifer (light) completely out of the context. The Aramaic word *ailel* means *to howl,* while the Hebrew word *helel* means *light* (or Lucifer). Lamsa's version has it, "How are you fallen from heaven! howl in the morning!" To Lamsa, the passage refers only to the King of Babylon.

Luther's German Translation

Martin Luther (1483-1546) once remarked that a good translation requires "a truly devout, faithful, Christian, learned, experienced, and practical heart." Little did the reformer know that God was preparing his own heart to fit that description. At the University of Wittenberg, Luther earned the *Baccalaureus Biblicus* degree in 1509 and the Doctor of Theology degree in 1512. Even when he published his own rendering of the Penitential Psalms in March 1517, Luther—who often humbly referred to himself as a "Doctor of the Sacred Scriptures"— entertained no serious thoughts of translating the entire Bible into his German dialect. On October 31 of the same year, he posted his famous 95 theses to the door of the Castle Church at Wittenberg. In the following year his translation of the Lord's Prayer and of Psalm 110 appeared.

God was guiding this pioneer a step at a time. Luther himself once explained that it was as if the Lord had His hand on his back, pushing him along—sometimes slowly, and often suddenly and swiftly, but always gently and purposefully. Quite confidently, the reformer could say, along with Abraham's servant, "I being in the way, the Lord led me." In 1519 Luther published his translation of King Manasseh's prayer and of Matthew 16:13-20. The year 1520 marked the appearance of his three most significant Reformation pamphlets: *An Address to the German Nobility; Concerning the Babylonian Captivity of the Church;* and *On the Freedom of the Christian Man.* On April 17 and 18, 1521, Luther stood before the emperor, the estates of the Empire, and the most important ecclesiastical prelates at the Diet of Worms, refusing to recant unless overcome by the Scriptures. For that reason, the reformer suddenly became a public outlaw. For Luther's immediate protection, the sympathetic elector, Frederick the Wise, "kidnapped" him and transported him to the Wartburg, a stately castle in the Thuringian forest overlooking Eisenach. Here during his friendly "house-arrest," Martin Luther providentially found his best (if not his only) opportunity of a lifetime to translate the Bible into German.

In November or December 1521, Luther began his translation of the New Testament. Philip Melanchthon

Luther's German Translation

Martin Luther's German Bible. Luther's first complete German Bible appeared in 1534. This edition appeared in 1739. Luther's Bible was the first German classic which standardized the German language; his Saxon vernacular became predominant and thus became the basis of modern German.

Martin Luther's German translation. Title page of a Luther Bible printed in early America. German immigrants insisted that America's printing presses circulate their beloved version.

(1497-1560) helped with the Greek, using the recently-published second edition of Erasmus' text. In September 1522, at Wittenberg, Luther's German New Testament—*Das Newe Testament Deutzsch*—appeared. Because of the month of publication, it was called the *Septemberbible*—the September Bible. It sold for one and a half florins. The new Bible contained several woodcuts, but the name of the publisher or translator did not appear in this first edition. Within 60 years, however, no fewer than 70 well-identified editions were published.

The passage of the three witnesses (I John 5:7b-8a) did not appear in Luther's Bible until 1574-1575, when a Frankfort publisher inserted it for the first time—almost 30 years after Luther's death. The passage does not appear in a Wittenberg edition until 1596. Actually, the passage does not even appear in any of the most ancient manuscripts, not even in Jerome's Latin Vulgate (A.D. 404). It first appears in the revised Roman Catholic Vulgate of the Middle Ages. Under much ecclesiastical pressure (and against his better judgment), Erasmus finally included the passage in the third edition of his Greek text (1522).

Great scholars such as Melanchthon, Bugenhagen, and Aurogallus aided Luther with the Old Testament. He used the Masoretic text which Gerson Ben Mosheh had published at Brescia in 1494. (The very copy which Luther used is at Berlin.) In 1523 Luther's Pentateuch appeared. The historical and poetical books appeared in 1524—the prophetic books in 1532. The whole Bible, with the Apocrypha in an appendix, was finally published in 1534.

With biblical scholarship still in its infancy, Luther's Bible was certainly not a perfect translation. (No translation is perfect.) In fact, Luther later remarked that Job would have been more impatient with his translation blunders than with the long speeches of his own miserable "comforters." Luther's Bible, however, was the first German classic which standardized the German language. In Luther's day the confusing variety of German dialects, such as Hanoverian, Swabian, Bavarian, and Saxon, caused scholars to continue to rely upon the unchanging Latin. But Luther translated the Bible into his own German dialect; consequently, his Saxon vernacular became predominant, and thus became the basis of modern German. Therefore, in a real sense, Luther's Saxon translation became the German *textus receptus* (received text).

It was a "free" translation, but generally a true one; his famous interpolation of the word *alone* in Romans 3:28— *allein durch den Glauben*—(by faith alone)—is a good example of the way in which he "made Paul speak German." As the great champion of *sola fide* (faith alone), *sola gratia* (grace alone), and *sola Scriptura* (the Bible alone), Martin Luther displayed the beauty and the force of Saxon German. A contemporary called him the "German Cicero," who reformed not only religion but also language.

Undoubtedly, his Bible, which played such a significant role in German literature and in the biblical Renaissance and Reformation of the sixteenth century, was Luther's greatest contribution. During his lifetime, 11 editions and numerous reprints of Luther's Bible were published. He was constantly trying to improve it. An edition of 1541 contained so many errors that Luther himself had it suppressed from the public. (Even in Scandinavia, Luther's Bible became the basis for vernacular versions.) The first Bible in a European language printed in America was a Luther Bible. The volume came from the press of Christopher Saur, in Germantown, Pennsylvania, in 1743 and is often called the "First Germantown Bible." Of the 1200 copies printed, only about 150 have survived.

Glossary

Apocrypha The 14 books of the Septuagint and of the Latin Vulgate that both Jews and Protestants consider uncanonical because they are not a part of the Hebrew Scriptures. The Roman Catholic church accepts 11 of these books as canonical and includes them in its versions, such as the Douay Bible and the Jerusalem Bible.

autograph An original manuscript, as it was written or dictated by the author. In biblical studies the term usually refers to the original handwritten Scriptures.

canon Literally means "measuring rod." Applied to the Bible, the term refers to those books that have been "measured" and found satisfactory as the inspired and authoritative rule of faith and practice for believers.

Erasmus' Text Called the *Textus Receptus* (Received Text), this was the text type that Erasmus used in his editions of the Greek New Testament. The first edition, appearing in 1516, was the first printed Greek text to be published. It agrees closely with the Byzantine Text (or Majority Text) and does not include the oldest manuscripts that have since become available. The oldest manuscripts on which it relies date only to about the tenth or eleventh centuries. All English Bibles of the sixteenth and seventeenth centuries were based upon Erasmus' text.

facsimile An exact copy or reproduction.

folio A large sheet folded to make two leaves (four pages) of a book; a manuscript or book of the largest common size, usually about 15 inches in length.

Koine Greek The Greek dialect commonly spoken in the first century and used in the writing of the New Testament.

manuscript An ancient handwritten copy of a text.

octavo The page size obtained by folding a whole sheet of paper into eight leaves (16 pages), usually from 5 x 8 inches to 6 x 9 1/2 inches; a book composed of pages of this size or folded in this manner.

Papyrus The pith of the papyrus plant; in biblical studies, the term refers to a handwritten document made of papyrus pith that has been cut in strips and pressed into writing material. In the arid climate of the Middle East, such manuscripts have been preserved for centuries. Our word *paper* is derived from the same term.

quarto The page size obtained by folding a whole sheet twice to make four leaves (eight pages); a book composed of pages of this size or whose pages are folded in this manner.

Septuagint A Greek translation of the Hebrew Old Testament produced in the third and second centuries B.C.

Textus Receptus *See* Erasmus' Text.

transliterate To represent or spell letters or words in the corresponding characters of another language.

vellum A fine parchment made from the skin of an animal, such as a calf, lamb, kid, or even an antelope.

vernacular The standard native language or dialect of a country or region.

Vulgate The Latin translation of the entire Bible, made by Jerome between A.D. 380 and 404. Its name comes from the Latin phrase *vulgata editio* (common edition), since it was the most widely used version in the West during the Middle Ages.

Bibliography

Anderson, Christopher. *The Annals of the English Bible.* 2 vols. London: William Pickering, 1845.

Bruce, F. F. *The Books and the Parchments.* New Jersey: Fleming H. Revell Co., 1963.

_____. *History of the English Bible.* New York: Oxford University Press, 1978.

Butterworth, Charles C. *The Literary Lineage of the King James Bible 1340-1611.* Philadelphia: University of Pennsylvania Press, 1941.

Copinger, Walter A. *The Bible and Its Transmission.* London: Henry Southeran and Co., 1897.

Earle, Ralph. *How We Got Our Bible.* Kansas City, Missouri: Beacon Hill Press of Kansas City, 1971.

Greenslade, S. L., ed. *The Cambridge History of the Bible: The West from the Reformation to the Present Day.* Cambridge: Cambridge at the University Press, 1963.

Hoare, H. W. *The Evolution of the English Bible.* London: John Murray, 1902.

Jackson, Samuel Macauley, ed. *The New Schaff-Herzog Encyclopedia of Religious Knowledge.* 12 vols. New York: Funk and Wagnalls Company, 1903-1912.

Kenyon, Frederic G. *The Bible and Modern Scholarship.* London: John Murray, 1948.

_____. *The Text of the Greek Bible.* London: Duckworth, 1937.

Kooiman, Willem Jan. *Luther and the Bible.* Philadelphia: Muhlenberg Press, 1961.

McAfee, Cleland B. *The Greatest English Classic.* New York: Harper & Brothers, 1912.

MacGregor, Geddes. *A Literary History of the Bible.* Nashville: Abingdon Press, 1968.

May, Herbert Gordon. *Our English Bible in the Making.* Philadelphia: The Westminster Press, 1952.

Merle d'Aubigné, Jean Henri. *The Reformation in England.* 2 vols. London: The Banner of Truth Trust, 1971-72.

Pattison, T. Harwood. *The History of the English Bible.* Philadelphia: American Baptist Publication Society, 1894.

Pope, Hugh. *English Versions of the Bible.* St. Louis: B. Herder Book Co., 1952.

Price, Ira Maurice. *The Ancestry of Our English Bible.* New York: Harper & Brothers, 1956.

Robinson, George L. *Where Did We Get Our Bible?* New York: Doubleday, Doran & Co., 1929.

Robinson, H. Wheeler, ed. *The Bible in Its Ancient and English Versions.* Westport, Conn.: Greenwood Press, 1970.

Schaff, Philip. *History of the Christian Church.* 8 vols. Grand Rapids: Wm. B. Eerdmans Publishing Company, 1970-73.

Simms, P. Marion. *The Bible in America.* New York: Wilson-Erickson, Inc., 1936.

Tischendorf, Constantine von. *Codex Sinaiticus.* London: The Lutterworth Press, 1934.

Westcott, Brooke F. *A General View of the History of the English Bible.* New York: The Macmillan Co., 1916.

Index

Index